Learning Station Models for Middle Grades

Nancy J. Kolodziej

National Middle School Association
Westerville, Ohio

Printed in the United States of America.

April Tibbles, Director of Publications
Carla Weiland, Publications Editor
John Lounsbury, Editor, Professional Publications
Mary Mitchell, Designer, Editorial Assistant
Dawn Williams, Publications Manager
Marcia Meade-Hurst, Senior Publications Representative
Peggy Rajala, Publications & Event Marketing Manager

Library of Congress Cataloging in Publication Data

Kolodziej, Nancy J.
Learning station models for middle grades / Nancy J. Kolodziej.
p. cm.
Includes bibliographical references.
ISBN 978-1-56090-236-2
1. Middle school education--Activity programs--United States. 2. Middle school teaching--United States. I. Title.
LB1623.5K65 2010
373.139--dc22
2009049587

National Middle School Association
4151 Executive Parkway, Suite 300
Westerville, Ohio 43081
1-800-528-NMSA f: 614-895-4750
www.nmsa.org

Contents

1

Why Use Learning Stations?

After teaching first grade for eight years, I decided that I needed a significant change of grade levels. So I accepted a position teaching seventh and eighth grade reading at a local middle school. Because I was the new teacher, I had to travel from classroom to classroom with a cart laden with all my supplies. My status as a roaming teacher and my naiveté about teaching adolescents led me to start with a traditional teaching style. I lectured about each topic while my students took notes and then completed worksheets. While I attempted to implement some games, cooperative learning, and readers' workshops, I had quite limited success in these endeavors and became frustrated with my students' lethargic behavior and indifferent attitudes. Behavior management—or shall I just say discipline—became a troublesome task. Had I made a wrong decision switching from first grade to middle school?

While struggling through that first year, I reflected often upon the differences between middle school students and first graders. It had been relatively easy to motivate young children and establish a successful classroom management program. Why was I struggling so much with this new age group? In search of answers, I read books such as Pipher's (1994) *Reviving Ophelia*, Atwell's (1998) *In the Middle: New Understandings About Writing, Reading, and Learning*, numerous journal articles, and National Middle School Association's position statement *This We Believe* (2003). I learned about adolescents' unique status of being "in the middle of everything . . . especially in the middle of changes—emotional, physical, psychological, and intellectual" (Atwell, p. 55). It is during this middle stage that they "undergo more rapid and profound personal changes between the ages of 10 and 15 than at any other time in their lives" (National Middle School Association, 2010, p. 5).

As I learned about the uniqueness of adolescents, I also came to recognize that in many ways these students were similar to first graders: neither group took to didactic teaching; they misbehaved when they were frustrated or bored. They thrived, however, on social interaction. Hands-on, interactive instructional activities such as I provided for first graders was, I realized, ideal for young adolescents.

The sense of disconnect that I felt with the majority of these middle school students was intensified because of my frontal teaching style. It was difficult to try to get to know 125 students when I spent so much class time talking *at* students. I began to consider techniques I used with my first graders that I thought would best meet the needs of my middle school students and help me get acquainted with each one as a distinct individual. The answer became quite clear: the use of learning stations would accomplish these goals. Learning stations are simply places with materials provided on a particular topic where a small group of students can go to engage in activities provided. After wholeheartedly instituting learning stations in my middle school classroom, I became much more successful. My hope is that this book will provide you with both the information and the motivation needed to help establish your version of learning stations in your classroom.

Adolescents' unique physical, social, and intellectual needs

Adolescents have unique physical and social needs (Van Hoose, Strahan, & L'Esperance, 2009) that are often not met in a traditional classroom. During a growth spurt that generally spans across two years of adolescence, a typical boy grows 4.1 inches, and an average girl grows 3.5 inches per year (Huebner, 2000). In addition, during this developmental stage the individual's bone formation is at its peak (Committee on Nutrition, 1999), and ossification, or hardening of the bones begins. Incredibly, prior to this age, these children did not even possess kneecaps, which form during a period of months during the adolescent stage (Van Hoose, Strahan, & L'Esperance, 2009). Hormonal changes are also taking place during these years, which often result in massive doses of adrenaline being released at inopportune times—such as in the middle of a test. These phenomenal changes in their bodies cause adolescents to squirm in their typically rigid school chairs. They often feel "achy" and have difficulty sitting still as they are characteristically expected to do.

Social needs. The social needs of young adolescents require our consideration, for they are a top priority in their lives. A common scene in my home is my adolescent daughter with a cell phone in one hand responding to instant messages on the computer with her other hand. Adolescents have a driving need to interact with their peers and be part of a social group. "It seems that being part of a group is more important than which group" (Powell, 2005, p. 39). This need to socialize "plays a major role in the psychological process, as it is influenced by, and interrelated with, physical, intellectual, and emotional development" (p. 38). A traditional middle school classroom setting provides limited time for peer interactions—and such interactions are often frowned upon in many classrooms.

Although adolescents often portray a strong sense of autonomy, they actually yearn for interactions with adults—other than their parents. As they hang in limbo between their childhood and adulthood, they try to find a sense of belonging in the adult world. Close relationships with adult figures fulfill this need, and teachers are often the adults chosen (Van Hoose, Strahan, & L'Esperance, 2009). Consider times when students seemed to want to "hang out" in your classroom and engage in "adult" conversations. These were their attempts to meander into the adult world.

When individuals interact, the primary vehicle of that interaction is language; and language and cognition are interrelated. This symbiotic relationship becomes very clear when individuals learn something new and complex. For example, when you first learned how to drive, you probably verbalized the process as you "put the key in the ignition," "checked the parking brake," and so on. Vygotsky (1962; 1978) theorized that language is the central mechanism of learning, and social interactions are necessary in order to internalize this learning. Thus, fulfilling adolescents' need to socialize positively affects their academic achievement. In fact, "On-task interaction with peers is more conducive to actualization of learning potential than on-task interaction with adults, because the presence of peers is more effective in motivating search and discovery, exchange of ideas, and feedback" (Ben-Ari & Kedem-Friedrich, 2000). Middle level teachers need to provide students with opportunities to verbalize their thoughts while learning in a socially interactive environment.

Individual needs. Each individual adolescent has his or her own specific strengths, needs, and learning style. In *The Differentiated Classroom: Responding to the Needs of All Learners,* Carol Ann Tomlinson (1999) makes an analogy between the Little Prince's taming of the lion to teachers' "taming" of students (p. 31). This taming involves getting to know each student as a distinct individual. Once a teacher possesses this invaluable knowledge, he or she can use it to plan and guide the instruction that will meet each student's individual needs.

Because of their varied personal and social needs, young adolescents respond well to using learning stations. They provide opportunities for informal social interaction;

they give students a chance to assume responsibility for their learning; they provide for collaboration and peer-to-peer teaching; they offer some choices; they use varied materials in various formats; they provide immediate feedback; they provide some physical movement; and they provide connections between varied subject areas. All in all, learning stations are, it could be said, developmentally responsive!

But I don't have time for this!

Teachers often claim that they don't have time to incorporate interactive learning into their classrooms. Rather, they feel pressured to deliver a deluge of information in an effort to meet a multitude of learning standards in preparing their students for state assessments. Although such instruction may seem like a reasonable approach, the vast majority of education experts and every one of the major national educational organizations; i.e., National Council of Teachers of Mathematics (2000), National Science Teachers' Association (2003), National Council of Teachers of English (2006), National Council for the Social Studies (1991), National Middle School Association (2005), and the International Reading Association and the National Middle School Association (2001) advocate an interactive, hands-on approach to learning rather than a teacher-as-dispenser-of-knowledge, textbook- and workbook-driven mode.

An interactive, hands-on approach engages and motivates students. They become responsive and eager to participate in learning experiences while developing a love for learning that will last a lifetime. We must make time for this strategy!

2

Putting Learning Stations into Operation

Planning and operating learning stations requires considering many factors, including meeting standards, differentiating instruction, assessing and evaluating student work, developing ideas for stations, developing materials, and establishing routines.

How do I meet the standards?

When visiting a classroom to observe a teacher candidate, I sat with Mr. Walters, the supervising teacher, at the back of his sixth grade classroom. The students' excitement as they eagerly entered the room and prepared for the start of class caught my attention. When the candidate began teaching a hands-on science lesson about magnetic poles, a couple of the students continually showed Mr. Walters their findings and related this activity to a scientific concept they had learned previously. When asked why his students had such genuine enthusiasm toward learning in this classroom, Mr. Walters attributed it to his involving students in engaging hands-on activities. As he reviews topics and concepts, he continually connects them to the activities that involve an active demonstration. He said, "When students encounter these concepts on the test, they remember vividly what happened during the activity." Not only is Mr. Walters preparing his students for state assessments, but more important, he is instilling a lifelong love of learning in his students.

By establishing learning stations in your classroom, you, too, can foster an excitement about learning while meeting the rigorous demands of your state standards. In fact, learning stations can enhance your students' attainment of academic goals while providing the opportunity for social interaction and a high level of student engagement. Incidentally, each of the sample stations included in this text is linked to a specific content area's national standards, which are identified.

Track standards coverage. I found that creating a chart of the state standards or performance indicators for your subject and grade level can be effective. Add a column to this chart to record dates on which you address each standard or performance indicator. As you plan activities, record the date the lesson will be implemented in the last column. As the school year progresses, this chart will help you determine which standards have been aggressively addressed and where potential gaps lie. Subsequently, you can adjust planning and instruction to meet these gaps.

Extension and review. Stations are particularly effective in expanding upon and reviewing challenging content or processes. When state assessment results indicated that our students experienced difficulty with vocabulary, a common station in my classroom became the Vocabulary Station. Although the activities in this station varied, terms with which students struggled frequently reappeared within the context of these activities.

Stations also effectively provide content review prior to the administration of your state assessment. Rather than providing drill and practice in a traditional worksheet format, you can review the difficult concepts in an engaging context to get your students actively involved in the review. (See the Science: Magic Square Vocabulary station, p. 59, for an example. The Social Studies: Vocabulary Word Sort station, p. 68, could also be used as a review rather than as an introduction as it is presented here.)

Where can I get ideas for stations?

Most of my ideas for learning stations came from my observations of students during lessons and ideas I generated. When I reflected upon my first year of middle school teaching, I recall that students usually dreaded the standards-required skill of outlining. I had provided students with numerous skill-building worksheets to develop their expertise in outlining. It was obvious that my students were bored and viewed outlining as pure drudgery. Therefore during subsequent years, I decided to use a developmentally appropriate learning station approach to meet this standard. In these stations, I incorporated hands-on activities relevant to students' lives. Following is a list of the resulting stations and a brief overview of each.

1. ***Outlining with Real Objects***—Designed to develop skill in determining main ideas and details, materials in this station included a bucket of "artifacts" I gathered from my house including pens, pencils, paper clips, plastic fruits, and pieces of Barbie doll clothes. Students, using the directions provided, established categories and then created a physical outline of the objects on the floor. Using laminated paper strips, they added a title, main ideas, and numerals and letters.

Student Directions:

Using Real Objects to Create an Outline

- You will work as a group to create an outline using the objects provided.
- Find a place on the floor to work.
- Take out all of the objects and the sentence strips. Sort through the objects to determine some of the possible main ideas. There are no "correct" main ideas. Instead, your group should figure them out.
- Create an outline of the real objects. Use the long sentence strips to write the main ideas and the short ones to write the Roman numerals, letters, and Arabic numerals. Place the objects in the outline instead of writing the names of the objects.
- Once you have finished the outline using the items, have your teacher check it and then copy it onto plain, lined paper. (Of course you will need to write the names of the objects or draw pictures of the objects on this written outline.) Each person in the group will need to hand in an outline. Be sure to give your outline a title.

Our Outline of Real Objects

I. (Write main idea or category here.)
 A.
 B.
 C.
II. (Write main idea or category here.)
 A.
 B.
 C.
 D.
III. (Write main idea or category here.)
 A.
 B.

2. ***Clay Outline Format***—This station was designed to help students understand when to use capital and lowercase letters, Roman and Arabic numerals, and periods while reinforcing the concept of parallel construction. Using clay strips, students created an outline format without any text on the floor.

Student Directions:

Clay Outline Format

I. Work as a group.
   A. Create one format as a group.
   B. All group members must help.

II. Task
   A. Create an outline format.
      1. Use many levels.
      2. Use parallel construction.
      3. You are only making the <u>frame</u> of the outline. There will be no information or text.
   B. Use clay.
      1. Make letters and numerals.
      2. Remember to include periods.

III. Scoring
   A. When complete, ask your teacher to score it.
   B. See the scoring guide below.

Scoring Guide

	Possible Score	**Your Score**
Parallel Construction	20	
Number of lines	20	
Number of levels	20	
Periods (one point off for each missing)	20	
Group's ability to work cooperatively	20	
	Total =	___________

3. ***Outlining Our Vocabulary Words***—As mentioned in the previous section, vocabulary was a district-wide emphasis; thus, the goal of this station was for students to apply their knowledge of vocabulary and their outlining skills by creating an outline that considered the relationships between the meanings of many of the vocabulary words taught thus far in the school year. As you can see in the word bank on the vocabulary word outline below, we focused our vocabulary study on roots, prefixes, and suffixes. Because I wanted students to retain previously taught vocabulary, our activities included a cumulative list of all words taught thus far. The students would have already worked with Lists 1-5, and in this cycle we were working on List 6. Students used the frame of the outline that was provided on the handout to get them started with their own outlines. I differentiated instruction by inserting different quantities in the blank in the second sentence in the directions on the handout.

Student Directions:

Vocabulary Station

You need two papers: this one and the List 6 vocabulary list. Complete the outline using all of the List 6 roots and at least _____ of the list 1-5 roots. Your main ideas should focus on the definitions of the roots. The outline is started for you. You will need to add several Roman numerals to complete the outline. If you run out of room, continue on the back of this paper.

Definitions of Root Words

I. Before
    A. Pre-
    B. ____________
II. Water: ______________
III. Numbers and quantity
    A. Numbers
        1. One
            a. ____________
            b. ____________
        2. Two: bi-
        3. Three: tri-
        4. Four: ____________
        5. Five: ____________
        6. Six: ____________
        7. Seven
            a. ____________
            b. ____________
        8. One hundred: __________

Word Bank for List 6

(Fill in your blank vocab list with these!)

de-	do the opposite of
alti-	high
centi-	100
dyna-	powerful
hexa-	six
hydro-	water
inter-	between
iso-	equal
cosmo-	universe
dia-	through

4. ***Outlining in Word: My Favorites***—To connect outlining with their personal lives and to learn computer outlining techniques, students working in pairs create outlines about their favorite things.

Student Directions:

Computer Station

Create an Outline Using MS Word™

You will create an outline using your favorite things as your main ideas and details. Do not put your real name on this paper, because other members of the class will be trying to guess who created this outline. Use a pseudonym (a false name) on your paper but use true information in the rest of your outline.

The title of the outline will be ________________________'s Favorite Things.

Identify your main ideas, subtopics, and the details. Examples of main ideas might be favorite foods, favorite books, favorite places, or favorite activities. You must have at least three levels (Roman numerals, capital letters, and Arabic numerals) in your outline.

1. Log onto the computer.
2. Go to the Start button, then Programs, and choose Word.
3. Change the font to size 12 or larger.
4. Choose the center text button and type the title for your outline.
5. Choose the left justify text button to begin your outline.
6. Begin typing your outline.
7. To indent and move to a lower level in your outline, press Tab.

Your outline may look similar to the one below. It does not have to be exactly the same

Title

I. Main idea
 A. Subtopic
  1. Detail
  2. Detail
 B. Subtopic
  1. Detail
  2. Detail
  3. Detail
  4. Detail
II. Main idea
 A. Subtopic
 B. Subtopic
  1. Detail
  2. Detail
III. Main idea

5. ***Outlining a Textbook***—To demonstrate that outlining is a useful study tool, students worked independently to outline a section of their social studies textbook. Main ideas are usually already identified by sideheads in the text.

6. ***Outlining Song Lyrics***—After listening to a popular song while following along with the printed lyrics, students created an outline based on the main idea and supporting details. This is not easy, but it is a task students readily attack.

Resources. In addition to creating stations based on your original ideas, a variety of resources can provide you with ideas that you can adapt for your classes. Verizon's Thinkfinity (http://www.thinkfinity.org/home.aspx) contains lesson plans in a searchable database for nearly every subject and grade level. Plans published on the site are linked to standards and are peer-reviewed to assure their quality. The "Student Materials" on the site include numerous interactive tools that students can manipulate. Discovery Education's website (http://school.discoveryeducation.com/lessonplans/) is another excellent resource for lesson plans. Although you may not find a multitude of plans written specifically for use in learning stations, you can easily adapt many of them for stations.

Is there a way to simplify planning?

To simplify your planning, keep certain station themes consistent but change the activities and content each time you use them. The following station themes were common in my classroom:

1. ***Listening:*** Books on tape, teacher-recorded material, and song lyrics were typically included. The song lyrics station was a student favorite. When possible (and after I screened them for inappropriate language and topics), I used songs that were popular among my students at that time. Lyrics are ideal for teaching literacy skills such as identifying main idea and theme, defining words using context clues, and making inferences. Lyrics may also be used to teach concepts in other curricular areas. For example, Billy Joel's *We Didn't Start the Fire* delineates historical events from 1949 to 1989. The band Alabama's *Song of the South* provides insights into the effects of the Great Depression on our culture.

To ease the financial burden of purchasing full-length CDs, virtually every song may now be purchased for a nominal fee from venues on the Internet such as iTunes. Be sure that you are downloading songs from a reputable and legal site. A list of such sites is available from Music United (http://musicunited.org/6_legalsites.html). Lyrics to songs may be found on many sites; simply search the Internet for "lyrics" and the title of the song (contained in quotation marks). As you plan your listening stations, keep copyright law in consideration. Another website (http://fairuse.stanford.edu/Copyright_and_Fair_Use_Overview/chapter7/index.html) outlines the copyright laws in relation to education use.

2. *Computers:* Internet sites, software, and webquests are among the options. Students may use utility programs, such as word processing, spreadsheets, and drawing tools to record data, write expository or narrative pieces, or to display creative ideas. Applets, such as those found on Utah State University's National Library of Virtual Manipulatives website (http://nlvm.usu.edu/en/nav/vlibrary.html) or Edinformatics' The Interactive Library (http://edinformatics.com/il/il.htm) provide excellent virtual hands-on math and science experiences.

3. *Writing:* An ideal station for a language arts classroom is a writing station, which is also well-suited for other content areas. Activities can include creating a children's picture book on a given topic, writing an editorial about a controversial topic for a local newspaper, assuming the role of a famous person and writing a speech when winning an actual or pretend award, and creating a comic strip explaining a process or historical event. The Math Curse station (p. 54) describes a writing station for a mathematics classroom.

4. *Independent work:* Although interactive and cooperative learning are vital elements in learning stations, a few assignments (both short-term and long-term projects) are best suited for individual work. The Outlining a Textbook Station was an independent workstation. Students assigned to this station sat at their own desks and outlined a section of the social studies textbook, which provided me an opportunity to conduct mini-lessons with some students.

How do I differentiate instruction?

Meeting the wide range of student needs and abilities in our classrooms can be a daunting task, particularly when whole-class instruction is the primary mode of delivery. National Middle School Association (2010) advocates differentiated instruction and states "Teaching approaches should capitalize on the skills, abilities, and prior knowledge of young adolescents; use multiple intelligences; involve students' individual learning styles; and recognize the need for regular physical movement" (p. 22). According to Tomlinson (1999), a teacher can differentiate content (what is taught), process (how a student will accomplish learning the material), or product (the finished piece that the student produces to demonstrate meeting the objective) based upon students' learning profiles (i.e. 504 accommodations or IEP's), interests, or readiness.

Learning stations provide many opportunities to differentiate any or all of these aspects. Suppose, for instance, that a social studies teacher was addressing the Learning Expectation "Understand the impact of individual and group decisions on citizens and communities" (6.01) from the Tennessee State Standard. "Personal development and identity are shaped by factors including culture, groups, and institutions. Central to this development are exploration, identification, and analysis of how individuals and groups work independently and cooperatively" (Tennessee Department of Education, 2001). The teacher could create several learning stations that would differentiate instruction in various ways. Student choice of stations would further differentiate instruction. Differentiated instruction possibilities are identified in chart form below.

Differentiated Instruction Possibilities

Learning/Assessment Activities	**What is differentiated?**			**To meet students . . .**		
	Content	Process	Product	Readiness	Interest	Learning Profile
Students may study decisions made by family groups, athletic teams, or world leaders.	X			X	X	X
Some students read books, others explore websites, and others conduct interviews.		X		X		X
Students demonstrate what they learned through dramatizing effects of a decision, writing a newspaper article about the effects of a political decision, or completing a teacher-created multiple choice exam.			X	X	X	X

Gather data on differentiation needs. To gather information about students' interests and learning profiles, teachers can use interest inventories, questionnaires, and interviews. Several such instruments are available free online. To find them, conduct in Internet search for phrases such as "student interest inventory," and "learning styles inventory." Data gleaned from these instruments can be used to identify student interests and preferred learning styles. If several students indicate an interest in sports, then a sport could be chosen for a learning station theme. Similarly, if several students consider themselves auditory learners, stations using books on tape, audio interviews, and discussion among peers could be established.

Determine prior knowledge on topic. Prior to instruction, teachers can assess students' prior knowledge in relation to that topic or concept. For instance, when beginning a unit on India, the teacher could have students complete a KWL or a concept map of information that is already known. The cases that follow contain examples of each of these approaches. The information gained through such an activity would help determine any misconceptions, areas of in-depth background knowledge, and important concepts that are not yet known. The teacher can then plan instruction according to students' needs.

KWL chart

K	W	L
** India is on the continent of Asia.* *There are jungles there.* *The people can belong to various religions.* *Some Indians speak Hindu.* *Buddha is honored there.*	** What other land forms are there?* *How do their religions compare to Christianity?* *What other languages are spoken there?* *Can most people in India speak English?*	

* Possible Responses

Student Directions:

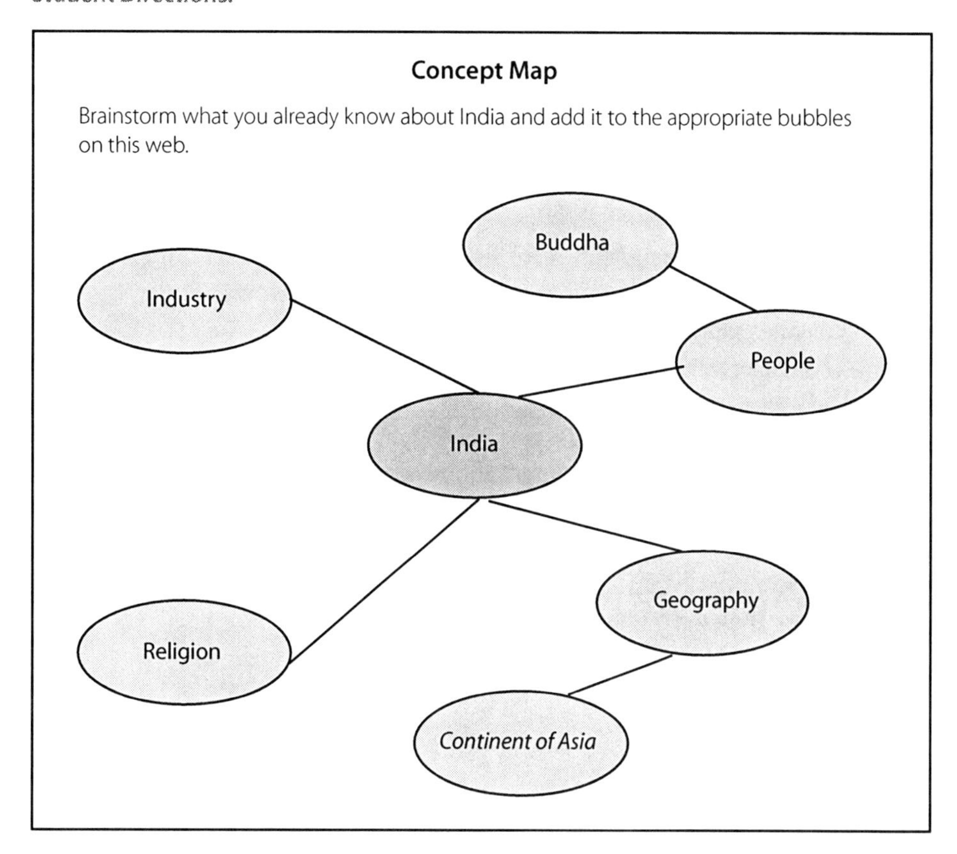

Consider literacy abilities. Also consider students' literacy abilities when differentiating instruction in learning stations. Supply a range of reading materials so that students may choose the ones that best match their interests and readiness. For example, one of my assignments focused on Dr. Martin Luther King Jr.'s "I Have a Dream" speech. Students had the choice of viewing the speech on streaming Internet video, reading the entire speech, or reading an excerpt from the speech. When given the choice of materials, most young adolescents will choose the one that best meets their needs unless the one at their level differs radically from their peers'. If students choose what looks easiest, discuss with them the benefits of using material at appropriate levels. Another option is to predetermine the materials for the students, thus eliminating student choice. Yet another option is to assign students to heterogeneous groups so that more competent students may assist struggling readers.

Consider ELL needs. Finally, when planning for learning stations, consider how to support English Language Learners (ELLs) who are more likely to be successful in learning English when provided with meaningful opportunities to interact with peers in a secure environment such as a small group. With learning stations, ELLs not only have more opportunity to verbally express themselves, but they can also quietly and easily seek clarification from their peers as needed. In addition, ELLs' academic achievement is enhanced when their learning activities incorporate the use of their native language (Teachers of English to Speakers of Other Languages, n.d.). By carefully considering group placement, teachers can provide these meaningful interactions for ELLs with peers fluent in English and when possible with peers of their native language. For more information about ELLs, explore the following websites:

Teachers of English to Speakers of Other Languages, Inc.
(http://www.tesol.org/s_tesol/index.asp)

Everything ESL
(http://www.everythingesl.net/)

The Internet TESL Journal for Teachers of English as a Second Language
(http://iteslj.org/)

How do I schedule stations?

When I taught in a self-contained classroom, my stations ran daily for 90 to 120 minutes during our guided reading time. In middle schools that do not schedule long blocks of time, however, it is difficult to incorporate most stations on a daily basis. Middle school classes need time for some direct instruction, ample discussion, and student presentations. Therefore, I planned my stations for times when small group or independent work was the best way to meet the objectives. Stations are a good way to introduce topics, such as discovering geometrical concepts, exploring properties of substances, or investigating characteristics of a particular country, artist, or genre. They also can be used to provide application or review of content that had been introduced in a whole-class format. The day following a cycle of stations, whole-class discussion usually concluded each topic so that students could both present and discuss station work.

Whole-class vs. stations. When deciding whether or not to use some form of whole-class instruction or a station approach for sections of your unit, begin by considering the level of scaffolding or assistance students will probably need. When I began the outlining unit, for instance, I knew of critical background knowledge that students would need to successfully master this skill. Consequently, I began this unit by instructing the class in concepts and procedures related to outlining. After approximately three class periods of instruction and informal assessment opportunities to determine students' understanding of outlining, I determined that they were ready to practice. Thus, a six-day cycle of stations ensued followed by a whole-class session in which we reviewed what they had learned in the stations, including a traditional paper-and-pencil test on outlining.

Typical Work Schedule

<table>
<tr><td>5-10 minutes</td><td colspan="6">Whole Class: Warm-Up activity, attendance, check and set homework</td></tr>
<tr><td>25 to 30 minutes</td><td>Group 1
Station A</td><td>Group 2
Station B</td><td>Group 3
Station C</td><td>Group 4
Station D</td><td>Group 5
Station E</td><td>Group 6
Station F</td></tr>
<tr><td>5 minutes</td><td colspan="6">Wrap Up: Discuss station challenges, work habits, etc.</td></tr>
</table>

In middle schools with class periods of about 45 minutes, you can reasonably expect students to visit just one learning station per day. I posted a station schedule in a pocket chart. At the end of each class period, the index cards that list the group members' names would each be moved one place to the right. The card that had been in the far right position would move to the beginning of the row. Typically, I set up six stations for each topic and assigned four students per station. For six days, students would visit each of the six stations. At times, there would be more than six stations, and students could choose ones that met their interests or learning styles. Most times, though, the choices for students were contained within the station directions themselves. For example, the vocabulary station directions might begin with "As a group, choose one of the following activities: Play Tricky Fruits and Vegetables (see p. 36) or create a visual dictionary using Inspiration™ software." Where teams have control over a longer instructional block of time, scheduling time for learning stations is not a real problem, and many options are available.

How should students be grouped?

There is no best way to group students. Grouping should be determined by a number of factors including learning goals, social considerations, behavior concerns, and language needs. Your basis for grouping will not necessarily be the same in each class. I strongly believe students should be heterogeneously grouped, unless there is a solid rationale for occasionally grouping homogeneously. Heterogeneous grouping allows strong readers to assist those who have difficulty reading. Creative and artistic students can stimulate idea generation for the group's skit, poster, or other craft assignment. Students who possess strong logical thinking skills may provide new insights in solving a mathematics problem or conjecturing a scientific hypothesis. In contrast, homogenous groups tend to be static, with less interaction among peers. Groups should be changed periodically so that all students will have opportunities to work with all other individuals.

Students self-select groups. As the year progressed, I would often let students create their own groups. Pieces of paper simply labeled "Group A," "Group B," etc., were posted. Each paper was numbered with the number of students I wanted in each group, usually four. Signing up for a group often resulted in friends' being in the same group. Because I told them that the ability to choose groups for subsequent station cycles was dependent upon their behavior during these self-selected groups, the student-created groups were often my best-behaved and most productive. Self-selection of groups was one the best classroom management incentives that I have ever discovered.

How or where do I set up stations in the classroom?

A large classroom with tables and chairs is ideal for conducting learning stations, but most classrooms are small and do not have tables. One solution is to place all of the materials for a station in baskets and place all baskets in one central location. Students may pick up the basket for their assigned station and find a place to work—on the floor, by moving desks together, or even out in the hall. Organize handouts in a paper sorter with generic titles on the shelves, such as "Station A," so that students can obtain handouts independently.

After my year of traveling from room to room with a cart, I was given a very large classroom. This room provided me enough space to have permanent areas for learning stations. The following year, however, I was moved to a very small classroom (see samples, pp. 19, 20). I had room to set up a permanent listening station and a station consisting of a row of three computers, but I used the "basket approach" for the remaining stations. Often, I would use the school library as a learning station location; students would pick up their station baskets and report to the library to work on tasks that required the use of that facility. Be sure to make arrangements with your school librarian so that he or she knows to expect your students and is aware of the assignment.

In addition to the room layouts that I used, there are many other ways to set up your classroom for learning centers. One simple way is to place student desks in groups of four, using each grouping as a learning station location. Some relatively small stations can be placed on window sills or even hung on a clothesline. The use of magnets and pocket charts can facilitate the placement of stations on file cabinets, doors, and walls.

Diagram of Large Classroom

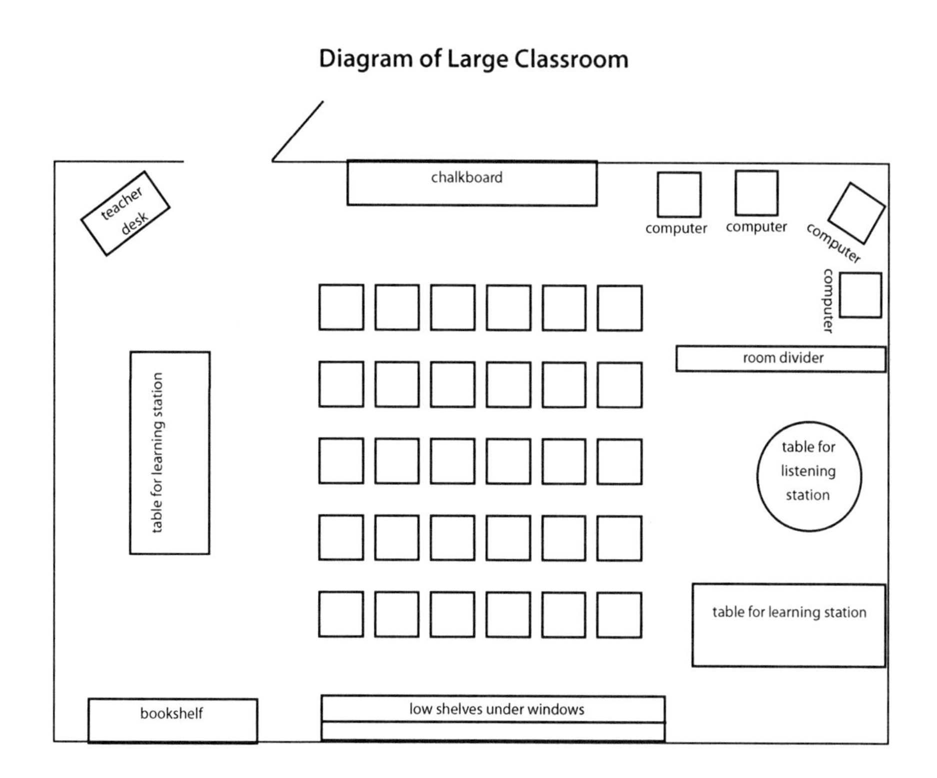

Diagram of Small Classroom

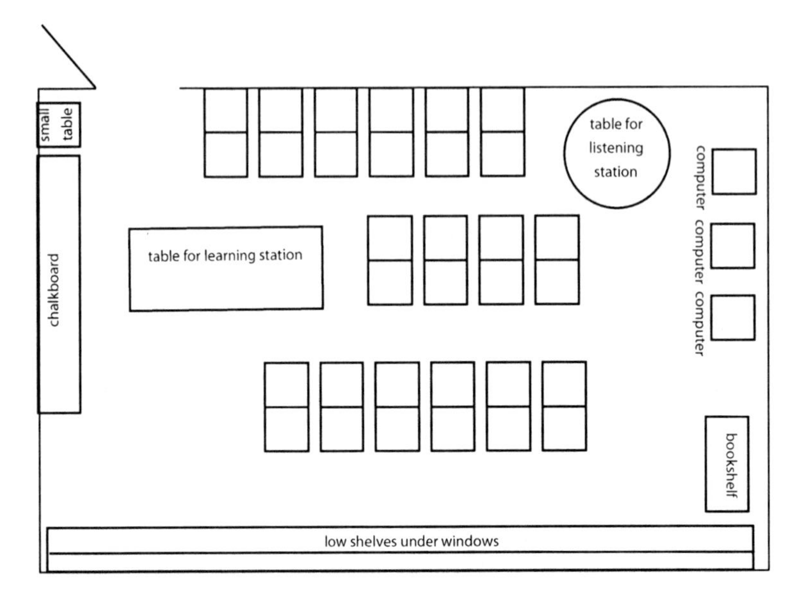

How do I assess and evaluate student work?

Assessment involves ongoing data gathering and analysis used both to advance learning and to determine students' progress towards meeting stated objectives. Evaluation, on the other hand, makes a judgment on what has been learned or produced. Learning stations readily involve both assessment and evaluation. When contemplating how to measure students' progress, the question that remains in the forefront is "What is the purpose of gathering the data?" We do need to evaluate work in order to help arrive at the expected grade to convey to parents on report cards. This, however, should not be our primary purpose for gathering data. Instead, assessment measures should be used mainly to inform our instructional practices. A student performance on a particular assessment helps us identify what that student has mastered and what additional practice or instruction is needed.

Managing, assessing, and evaluating student work produced during station time is no small task. The following ideas and suggestions can make this task manageable.

1. *Create anecdotal record folders to record observations and student instructional needs.* I used color-coded file folders for each class that corresponded to where I placed materials to be checked. Inside the folders create an index card for each student, tape the cards in an overlapping manner in columns; then you

can flip to select the one you want. Keep the folder handy during each period so that you can easily record anecdotal notes about each student's struggles, accomplishments, and concerns.

2. *Establish a particular spot where students will always turn in papers.* I used stacking letter trays, available at any office supply store, and pocket folders. Each one of the letter trays was labeled for a particular class. Students would place completed papers in the appropriate tray. I kept a colored file folder (each period had its unique color) in each tray. After class, I would take the papers and place them in the left side of that class's folder. I could then easily gather up the folders to check papers at home or during personal planning time.

3. *Set up a routine for returning papers to students.* Once I checked papers, I returned them to the appropriate folder and placed them in its right-hand pocket. At the start of each class, I could look in that class's folder and return papers or ask a student to do this.

4. *Create a grading rubric when you establish the station.* Include the rubric in the station materials so students have a clear picture of what is expected of them. If possible, go over the rubric with students before they begin work at the stations.

5. *Use assignments that produce a product that can be assessed on the spot.* Use a temporary record sheet that you can carry with your anecdotal notes folder. Later, you can transfer them to your grade book.

6. *Pair students.* When students complete a handout, they discuss it with each other and reach consensus. Then, they each fill in their agreed-upon response. After completing them, the pair staples their papers together. Randomly decide which one (the first or second paper) you will grade for all stapled sets. Be sure to stick with your choice so that students can't claim bias. Here are the directions given for such an assignment.

Student Directions:

Paired Assignment

1. You will work with a partner for this assignment.
2. Read the passage about Dr. Martin Luther King, Jr.
3. After reading the passage, discuss its main idea and supporting details and come to an agreement about your thoughts.
4. Make a web showing the agreed upon main idea and supporting details.
   Each person must make a web.
5. Staple your web to your partner's.
   I will randomly select one of the two webs to grade; therefore, both webs should be of the same high quality.

How can I integrate the curriculum?

The middle school movement has advocated moving away from the traditional separate subject curriculum. In a position statement on curriculum integration, National Middle School Association (2002) said: "We must encourage middle level educators to push themselves beyond the conventional, separate subject format and to expand their use of integrated curriculum formats ranging from intra-team planning of interdisciplinary units at a basic level to more advanced implementation of full-scale, integrative programs in democratic classrooms" (p. 1). Two examples to do this with learning stations are found on the following pages.

Curriculum mapping for integration. Using literacy stations provides an ideal opportunity for correlating two or more subjects. Heidi Hayes Jacob's (1997) curriculum mapping technique is a highly effective procedure to use in planning for cross-curricular integration. "The curriculum mapping spreadsheet of what is taught and when it is taught over the course of a year reveals potential areas for concurrent or correlated teaching of a topic or process as well as opportunities for interdisciplinary unit design" (Jacobs, 2000, p. 28). Teachers put upcoming topics, skills, and assessments on a calendar. Then they share those calendars with their teammates to identify places where they can collaborate and move toward integrating the curriculum.

Example: If you compared your social studies map with the language arts teacher's map, you might notice some connections that would, to a degree, integrate the two subjects. For instance, by moving your anticipated treatment of the Great Depression from January to November when her class will be reading the novel *Esperanza Rising*, the work in the two classes will be mutually supportive. In your social studies class, you can plan a learning station about the increase of migrant workers resulting from the Great Depression, which ties in perfectly with a main conflict in the novel. Furthermore, rather than simply studying migrant farming camps in general, you have students study Weedpatch Camp, which was a primary setting of the novel. In Spanish class, students could make further connections by learning vocabulary for fruits and vegetables from the novel. Such a multidisciplinary approach would help students make connections between subject areas and understand the content better.

The integrative approach. If you are in a school that is organized by teams, you can expand beyond a *multidisciplinary* approach and collaborate with your colleagues to implement the more complete *integrative* approach advocated by Beane (2002). Beane's democratic view of curriculum development hinges on the concept that students help develop the year's curriculum when teachers ask them two key questions: "What questions or concerns do you have about yourself? What questions or concerns do you have about the world?" (p. 26). After generating responses, students work to group them into conceptual themes, which become the basis of the year's curriculum across all content areas. Rather than a narrow, subject-based topic such as the Great Depression, these themes are broad concepts that invite exploration, such as power, change, freedom, innovations, and poverty.

Example: Suppose your students have chosen the theme of conservation. In math class, students may work at stations to apply statistics to explore topics of their choice related to conservation. In language arts, one station may prompt students to create a dramatic story about deforestation while students explore the effects of deforestation in science class. In social studies, students might explore the need for, and efforts toward, conservation in a self-selected geographical area. The possibilities are endless, and the outcome is that students experience "the democratic way of life . . . [by connecting] self-interest and the common good . . . [and] involve students in activities to understand themselves, one another, and the world around them" (Beane, 2002, p. 26).

These are very brief explanations of curriculum mapping and curriculum integration. For more thorough treatments, consult Jacobs' book *Mapping the Big Picture: Integrating Curriculum and Assessment K-12* (1997), Erb's *This We Believe in Action,* Chapter 10 (2005), Beane's *Curriculum Integration: Designing the Core of Democratic Education* (1997), and Springer's *Soundings: A Democratic, Student-Centered Education* (2006).

What is my role when students work in stations?

Being accessible while students are working in the stations gives you incredible opportunities to work one-on-one or with small groups. Roaming among students during station time and engaging in brief conversations helps establish more personable relationships between teachers and students.

At first. When you first initiate learning stations in your classroom, it is important to monitor student behavior and progress at the stations. Don't plan to work intensively with a group of students at the outset; instead, use this initial time to set and reinforce expectations. Assume the role of observer, and occasionally, facilitator. The goal is to have students function independently and take charge of their own learning.

Small group and individual instruction. Once your students understand the expectations and the routines of station time, you can begin to meet with small groups or individuals for mini-lessons. Use data from assessments and your anecdotal notes to determine what mini-lessons are needed and by what students. Keep these lessons brief (5 to 9 minutes) and focused on specific objectives. For example, while observing students working at your Outlining With Clay station (p. 44), you notice that Tom is having difficulty understanding the order in which to use Roman numerals, capital letters, Arabic numerals, and lower case letters. You noted this on his card in the anecdotal record folder. Throughout the cycle of the station, you note similar comments about a few other students. Subsequently, you plan and conduct a mini-lesson to reteach the order of bullets in outlining to this small group of students.

How do I maintain student behaviors during stations?

Many middle level teachers are reluctant to implement learning stations based on their apprehension related to classroom management. Because my first year of teaching at the middle level was so challenging, I confess I was a little apprehensive about implementing learning stations in my seventh and eighth grade classrooms. I worried about behavior management, particularly with keeping students on task.

I also wondered if my students would consider stations to be too juvenile for their age level. I would soon learn my concerns were unfounded as apprehension turned to ecstasy. Learning stations, have a very positive effect on student behavior and the overall classroom environment, due in part to increased student engagement.

The first major indication I had about the success of the stations was conveyed by David, an eighth grader who had challenged my authority since the first day of school. He was a reluctant student and visibly and regularly displayed his disinterest in school. Each day, David would saunter into class and make evident his detachment from classroom academic activities. The day after I began using stations, David appeared at my classroom door and asked, "Are we doing stations today?" After I replied affirmatively, David did a fist pump and let out a strong and enthusiastic, "Yes!" Smiling, he entered the room and sat down ready to begin. It was a major turning point for both of us. David no longer challenged me and even put moderate to enthusiastic effort into completing assignments throughout the rest of the year.

David was not, by any means, the only student whose motivation was increased as a result of learning stations. Throughout my remaining three years teaching middle school, numerous students wrote on end-of-the-year class evaluations that my class was their favorite, and the most commonly cited reason was my use of learning stations. When students are passive, they become bored and are likely to act out; but when students are motivated and engaged in learning, discipline problems are minimized.

In addition, I discovered that the camaraderie in my classroom inspired positive behaviors and respectful interactions. As they work in learning stations, students become more adept at working through social problems without the involvement of the teacher. The result of all this is a more cohesive and positive learning community.

The one-on-one opportunities provided by learning stations can help squelch attention-seeking behaviors. Once stations begin, a teacher can spend a couple of minutes defusing a student who arrives in class angry because of a hallway incident. Students begin to realize that if they need a teacher's attention, they can get a few minutes of one-on-one time during stations.

Although I paint a rosy picture, I certainly experienced some difficulties. I often used stations as an incentive to behave. If a class acted up, I would tell them that the disruptive behavior needed to cease, or we would delay our use of stations. After experiencing such a delay, their cooperation and behavior improved significantly. A few times when the majority of students were not meeting behavior expectations during stations, I simply stopped all groups, sent them back to their own seats, told them the reason I had halted station activity, and provided an alternate assignment for the rest of that period. The next day, before sending students to stations, I reminded them of previous infractions, and there were rarely behavior problems that day.

Getting started: Establish routines. Prior to implementing stations in your classroom, establish explicit routines and expectations. Students should know what to do when they walk in the classroom, how to move about the room, and what to do as dismissal time approaches. At the start of each class, my routine was the same regardless of whether or not we would be doing stations that day. Students entered the room, moved their own wooden sticks to the "present" can to record their attendance for the day, placed any papers to be handed in into the appropriate slot, and began work on the "warm-up activity" as soon as the bell rang.

Establishing attention-getting cues is also a necessary precursor to implementing stations. I taught students three different cues: lights out, count of three, and "executive hats." This last technique was one I used with my first graders, although I called it "listening caps." To initiate students' response, I would say "executive hats" or simply strike the pose myself. The pose is simply folding hands on top of the head (as an executive may demonstrate when in serious thought). The rule is that once the students' hands are on their heads, they cannot speak. I was hesitant to try this technique with my middle school students because I thought they would consider it "babyish," but I was pleased to see that it worked very effectively with the seventh grade students. Eighth grade students were a little reluctant, so I rarely used it with them. The bonus of the technique is that when students place their hands on their heads, they cannot fiddle with station materials, type on the keyboard, or otherwise engage in off-task behavior.

Modeling expectations. Once you have firmly established these routines, you are ready to set the stage for stations. Begin by telling students that you will be giving them more responsibility for their own learning while providing them with opportunities to interact with one another. Most students have been exposed to some form of learning stations in the elementary grades, so you could ask them about their memories of using stations. Share with them your high expectations for quality of work and positive interactions and relate the already established classroom rules to stations.

To explicitly demonstrate your expectations for student behavior during stations, set up one simple station at which students can easily succeed without any assistance from you. For modeling purposes, this station should take about 10 minutes to complete. Review the routine they should follow each time they begin a new station. Your routine may be similar to the following:

1. Move to your station's work area.
2. Make sure everyone in your group is present.
3. If you need to get supplies for your station, choose one person to retrieve them.
4. Read the station directions for this particular station.
5. Begin to work.
6. When you are finished, straighten up your station and put any completed work in the appropriate place.
7. Return to your regular seat.
8. If you finish before others, turn to your independent work or read your SSR book.

Consider posting your routine until students know it well. After discussing the routine, choose a group of four or five students to work at the station while the rest of the class observes and takes notes about the group and individual processes demonstrated. After the group completes the station, members return to their seats and discuss the class's observations. Although you may feel that giving up instructional time to model the use of stations will be questionable, it is well worth the time spent and will result in less wasted time in the future.

If your students have not worked in groups very often, the first day that all students work at stations, use the same lesson plan for all the stations to simplify setup and cleanup times and to allow for whole-group time to explain about the direction sheet. As students work, circulate among them, reinforcing positive behaviors and progress.

Maintaining desired behaviors. Place the responsibility for maintaining desired behaviors in the students' hands. They can self-assess their work habits and also assess those of their peers. Rubrics, such as the one below, can be used. Promote student autonomy by writing sufficiently explicit student directions for each station. Students should read the directions and attempt to follow them before they ask for oral directions.

Student Directions:

Rubric for Self-Assessing Behaviors in Stations

Student ______________________ Date ______________

Behavior Skill	Never	Rarely	Most of the time	Always
Listens to others				
Responds appropriately				
Respects others' opinions				
Follows directions				
Performs role in team				
Accepts responsibility for actions				
Remains on task				
Allows others to remain on task				
Successfully contributes to team product				

Any information that you want to share with teacher:

____

In the assessment section (p. 20) I discussed the use of the anecdotal notes folder. This tool, or something similar, can help you manage behavior during stations. After teaching students study skills (organization, listening skills, note taking, etc.) and demonstrating the characteristics of a middle school student with strong study skills, I told students that they would be assessed each marking period for their own study skills. They began each marking period with a grade of 100%, and would retain that grade unless they demonstrated lack of study skills. From that point on, as I circulated during learning stations I could subtract points from this grade when necessary. Actually, I rarely subtracted points. If I saw some students who seemed to be off task, I'd loudly say, as if to myself, "I think it's time to consider skill behaviors" and hold my anecdotal notes folder in clear sight. Mention of this forthcoming observation was usually enough to get students back on track.

Last words of advice. Using learning stations as one means of promoting learning is rewarding and energizing. It is a joy to see enthusiastic and engaged middle school students working cooperatively to achieve goals. The ability to connect with students and meet their individual needs is invaluable. Planning and organizing learning stations may be time-consuming, especially at the outset, and there will be glitches along the way. In the long run, however, your students will benefit academically and socially, and you will know that you have made a positive difference in their lives.

3

Standards-Based Learning Stations

This section provides several sample learning stations that will give you ideas of what is possible. All of them relate directly to cited standards. Most of them can be completed in one class period, but others may require additional time. You may be able to use some of them with only minor changes, while other examples will serve as springboards for generating ideas that will meet the particular needs of your students. Also look at the stations for possibilities in other curricular areas, for while the content of a sample lesson may differ from your discipline, the station's format, instructions, or methods can apply in any content area or in multidisciplinary approaches. Once you start planning stations, new ideas will come easily, and the possibilities for learning stations will bring a new excitement to your classroom.

ART

Art station: Guess my artwork

Related to Arts Education Achievement Standard

2.3: Students select and use the qualities of structures and functions of art to improve communication of their ideas. (Consortium of National Arts Education, 1994)

This station is based upon the game *Guess Who* (explained in the Directions Handout, p. 35), in which one player secretly chooses a character from among a number of given choices. His opponent asks a series of *yes* or *no* questions to eliminate possibilities until the opponent can guess the first players' chosen character. Rather than using characters and their traits, this station uses teacher-selected artwork and focuses the students on specific artistic elements. This station can be used throughout the year by changing the vocabulary terms on the student handout and the artwork on the playing cards to match content under study at the time.

Materials and preparation

1. ***Create the student handout.*** Begin by choosing vocabulary terms, perhaps using the ones listed in the handout on p. 34. The words were selected from Metropolitan Nashville Public School's *Visual Arts Academic Vocabulary Standards, Grades 7 & 8* (http://www.mnps.org/Page22556.aspx).

2. ***Create the playing cards.*** You will need at least two identical sets of 25 to 40 cards, one for the host and one for the group of players. If possible though, create enough sets of cards so that all group members at this station will have their own deck.

   a. To create the playing cards, first locate images of artwork on the Internet. To help select the artwork, use the vocabulary list that you created in step one. In other words, if you included the term *sepia*, some of your choices should include this color. Here are some sites that you will find beneficial:

      - Ibiblio's *Famous Artwork's Exhibition* (http://www.ibiblio.org/wm/paint/)

      - AbsoluteArt's *Art History Resources* (http://wwar.com/artists/)

      - Gary Kaemmer's *Famous Artists' Gallery* (http://www.famousartistsgallery.com/)

      - All Famous Artists' *Fine Art by Artists* (http://www.allfamousartists.com/buy-art-prints-posters.html).

   b. As you locate the images, save each one to your computer or flash drive. To save images, right-click on the image you want to save. A menu will appear in a pop-up window, and in this menu click on "Save picture as..." Then, in the Save Picture window, type a name for your picture and choose the location where you want to save it.) You could create a folder called *Playing Cards*, and save all of the pictures in that one folder.

c. The next step is to print the playing cards. Your printing method will depend upon your software and printer. One of the easiest ways to print your cards is to simply open the folder containing your images and right-click on one of the images. A Photo Printing Wizard window will likely open onto your screen. Follow the directions in that menu and choose to print in the 3.5 x 5" format. Alternately, you could use PowerPoint to print by placing each image on an individual PowerPoint slide. Then print the slides as *Handouts,* printing six slides per page, or print them directly onto index cards by changing your paper size in the printer settings. If you choose the first option, consider printing on card stock so that once you cut the cards apart, they will be more durable. Another useful tip is to print each set of cards on a different color card stock or index card. This makes it easy to keep the sets separate from one another.

d) Place each set of completed playing cards into its own zippered plastic bag.

3. ***Create the student directions*** (see sample, p. 35).

Assessment and evaluation

Collect the student handouts and use these data for a formative evaluation to determine terms that need further instruction. Accumulate a master list of the "Total for Each Term" column to evaluate the frequency of use of each vocabulary term. Terms that were used frequently are more fully understood by the students than those that were infrequently used. Consider reinforcing the vocabulary that was rarely used during whole-class instruction time or conduct mini-lessons for students who used few of the vocabulary terms.

Scoring Directions:

Guess My Artwork: Handout

Name____

- Before playing, review the terms that you are unsure of and write their definitions on the chart.
- Each time you ask a question that includes a term listed below, place a tally mark in the column for that round of play. Also, in each round, the first person to ask a question containing a term circles the "3" for that round and earns 3 points. The winner of each round circles "5' in the Bonus Points row.
- After you have completed the game, add your tallies for each term and then add that last column to determine your Grand Total.

Terms	Definitions	Round 1	Round 2	Round 3	Round 4	Total for Each Term
aerial perspective		3	3	3	3	
analogous colors		3	3	3	3	
asymmetrical balance		3	3	3	3	
blending		3	3	3	3	
caricature		3	3	3	3	
color scheme		3	3	3	3	
cross-hatching		3	3	3	3	
distortion		3	3	3	3	
elevation		3	3	3	3	
exaggeration		3	3	3	3	
gradation		3	3	3	3	
hatching		3	3	3	3	
hue		3	3	3	3	
intensity		3	3	3	3	
linear perspective		3	3	3	3	
montage		3	3	3	3	
one point perspective		3	3	3	3	
picture plane		3	3	3	3	
scale		3	3	3	3	
spectrum		3	3	3	3	
split complement		3	3	3	3	
technique		3	3	3	3	
tone		3	3	3	3	
two point perspective		3	3	3	3	
Bonus Points: The winner of each round wins 5 (circle if you are the winner)		5	5	5	5	
Round Totals						
GRAND TOTAL						

Student Directions:

Guess My Artwork

Have you ever played the game *Guess Who?* The format of this game is similar. One person plays the role of the host, and the other group members are contestants. The goal of the game is to try to guess the host's card by asking questions that use art-related vocabulary terms. Here are the rules of the game.

1. Each person takes a handout. Quickly review the terms. Write notes about those that are not familiar in the second column of the handout.
2. Each person takes a deck of playing cards. Be careful to keep each deck separate so that the decks do not become mixed up with one another.
3. Determine who the host of Round One will be.
4. The host places her cards face down in a pile and randomly chooses one card from that pile. The host looks at her card but does not show it to the other players.
5. The players lay out their cards so that they may easily view them all.
6. Moving in a clockwise manner from the host, each player takes a turn following these instructions:
   a. Ask a question about the host's card that will have a "yes" or "no" answer. If the question is not a yes or no question, the host refuses to answer it, and the player rephrases the question.
   b. Players guess by trying to use the terms on the handout in their questions. They earn a point each time they use a term. They may only use one term per question.
   c. The first player to use a term in a round earns three points instead of one, and they circle the "3" on the handout.
   d. Players eliminate art pieces based on the host's answers to questions.
   e. Each player may receive only one response per turn. After a player's one question has been answered, play proceeds to the next contestant.
   f. Example: a player asks, "Is the artist's use of scale true to life?" (Notice that this question can be answered with a yes or no response.) The host replies, "no." Then all players turn over all of the pictures in which the artist's use of scale is true to life.
7. When a player thinks he knows the host's secret card, he may ask if that is the host's card during his next turn. If he correctly guesses the card, he earns five bonus points (see the last row on the handout). If his guess is incorrect, he may not ask any other questions, and play proceeds to the next contestant.
8. At the end of a round, all contestants should add the tally marks in that round's column to determine their total for that round. The host of the game earns the same amount of points as the winner of that round.
9. At the end of the game, determine the total amount each term was used and write this in the right-hand column. In addition, determine your total number of points. The player with the most points wins.
10. Return your decks of cards to their bags and place your papers in the Papers Handed In slot.

Foreign language station: Tricky fruits and vegetables

Related to ACTFL Standard

1: Students understand and interpret written and spoken language on a variety of topics. (American Council on the Teaching of Foreign Languages, n.d.)

This simple game was enjoyed equally by first, seventh, and eighth graders. It can be used to review vocabulary terms in any subject area or to focus on pronunciation and translation of foreign language words as it is used here. To provide cross-curricular connections with literacy and connect to the novel *Esperanza Rising,* Spanish words for fruits and vegetables are the focus of this sample. The rules, though quite simple, can be confusing when the game is played for the first time. Prior to setting out this station, take about five minutes of whole-class time to model the game. Play against one student while stating aloud your thought processes. The following dialogue is an example of the conversation that might ensue when demonstrating this game. "T" refers to the teacher, and "M" refers to a student named Michelle:

T: To help you understand the rules of the game, I will play against Michelle, and I will verbalize my thoughts as I go. To begin the game I pick up the first card, turn it over, and read it aloud. I have the word "ciruelas." After pronouncing the word, I must also give its English translation which is "plums." My opponent could challenge me if I pronounced the word incorrectly, or if I didn't know the translation of the word. If I were wrong in the pronunciation or the translation, that card would be placed in the bottom of the deck, and my turn would be over. Because I had the correct answer, I get to put this card in my temporary pile. Now I need to decide if I'd like to try another word or if I want to end my turn now. I am going to play it safe and end my turn now. This means that the card currently in my temporary pile will now be moved to my permanent pile. I will never lose the cards that are in my permanent pile. Now it is Michelle's turn to go. So, for her turn to begin she needs to take a card from the pile.

M: I have "uvas," and I know that means grapes.

T: Class, show me thumbs up or down. Is Michelle correct?
(Students respond with a thumbs up.)

T: Who can tell Michelle where she should put her card?
(Students respond.)

T: Yes, she should place the card in her temporary pile. Now she can decide if she wants to draw another card or end her turn. If she ends her turn now, where will her card be placed?
(Students respond.)

T: Right, it will go into her permanent file, and she will keep that card in that pile for the rest of the game. What would happen if Michelle goes again and she picks up a blank card?
(Students respond.)

T: Yes, that's the tricky part of the game. When you pick up a blank card, you must forfeit all of the cards in your temporary pile. Remember that you will never lose the cards that are in your permanent pile. I think that we may now be ready to try to play the game.

Materials and preparation

1. Choose words for the game. You should have least 10—but more if possible.

2. Create word cards. You should have about 50 cards total, but the number does not have to be precise. So, if you chose 10 words in step one, make 5 cards of each word. If you chose 16 words, make 3 or 4 cards of each word. The repetition of the words will enhance students' retention. Use 3 x 5" index cards or card stock.

3. Create 5 blank cards of the same color and size as the word cards. Shuffle them randomly into the pile of word cards.

4. Place the cards in an envelope or small plastic bag.

5. Create a student handout listing all of the words that you put on your word cards (see p. 38). Note: With the exception of the Spanish vocabulary words, this handout was created in English so that all readers of this book would be able to read it.

6. Create the student directions (see sample, p. 39).

Assessment and evaluation

Students will note words that caused difficulty in the "Errors" column of their handouts. Use these data to determine words that need to be reviewed and students who may benefit from additional instruction.

Tricky Fruits and Vegetables Game Handout

Spanish Vocabulary	Errors (each time you make an error, place a check mark in the row of the troublesome word)
uvas	
higos	
guayabas	
melones	
cebollas	
almendras	
ciruelas	
papas	
aquacates	
esparagos	
duraznos	

Student Directions:

Tricky Fruits and Vegetables Game

SET UP

1. Take a Tricky Fruits and Vegetables Game Handout. Review the pronunciation and translation as a group.
2. Mix the cards up. (Be sure that the blank cards are mixed in.)
3. Place them upside down in a stack on the table.

THE PLAY

1. The player takes a card from the top of the stack.
2. He reads the word in Spanish and tells its English translation.
   a. If his pronunciation or translation is incorrect, the card goes to the bottom of the pile, and his turn is over. He should put a check mark in the "Error" column in that word's row on his handout.
   b. If his pronunciation and translation are correct, that card is placed in the player's temporary pile. Go to step 3.
3. The player decides whether to go again or stop.
   a. If he stops, he places all of the cards from his temporary pile into his permanent pile. He will never lose the cards from the permanent pile.
   b. If he goes again, he will choose another card and repeat steps 1-3 as many times as he chooses until he decides to stop or draws a blank card.
4. If the player draws a blank card, the player's turn ends and he must forfeit all cards in his temporary pile. (Place them at the bottom of the pile.)

THE WINNER

1. Game ends when all of the cards (except for blanks) are claimed or when time is up.
2. The player with the most cards wins!

CLEAN UP

1. Shuffle the word cards and place them back in the envelope.
2. Place your Tricky Fruits and Vegetables Game Handout in the Papers Handed In tray.

Health station: Public service messages

Related to National Health Education Standards:

1. *Students will Comprehend concepts related to health promotion and disease prevention to enhance health.*
2. *Students will Analyze the influence of family, peers, culture, media, technology and other factors on health behavior.*
4. *Students will Demonstrate the ability to use interpersonal communication skills to enhance health and avoid or reduce health risks.*
5. *Students will Demonstrate the ability to use decision-making skills to enhance health.*
8. *Students will Demonstrate the ability to advocate for personal, family and community health. (American Association for Health Education, 2007)*

In this station students critically review commercial advertisements for potentially negative outcomes that they can then present to classmates and other groups. After choosing and discussing a generic ad, student groups will each create a public service message expressing a negative outcome that young adolescents could experience as a result of the advertisement. Finally, each group will present its public service message to the class. If you only have a single period available, a period on another day will be needed.

Materials and preparation

1. Create the Student Directions (see sample, p. 41).
2. Create the Advertisement-Consequences Web (see sample, p. 42).
3. Create the Audience Guide (see sample p. 43).
4. Decide on the format for the student storyboards. An easy way to create a storyboard is to simply fold a paper into eight sections. Each frame indicates a segment of the message. Or, check out the many free templates available online. Karen J. Lloyd's Storyboard Blog (http://karenjlloyd.com/blog/free-storyboard-template-downloads/) has some free templates that would work well. Schoolhouse Video (http://www.schoolhousevideo.org/Pages/Storyboard.pdf) has one that may also meet your needs. To find additional resources, conduct an Internet search for "storyboard templates."
5. Create the grading rubric, possibly with students' help. Review it with students before they begin work at the station so that they are fully aware of expectations (see sample, p. 43).

6. You may want to collect magazines and newspapers for students to peruse in Step 1 of the Student Directions—having screened them for potential distractions.

Student Directions:

Public Service Messages

The purpose of advertising it to persuade consumers to assume certain viewpoints that will influence them to purchase certain products. Unfortunately, experiencing some advertisements increases the likelihood we will engage in behaviors that can harm our health. Consider television, radio, magazine, electronic, and billboard advertisements.

Your task is to choose an advertisement that could negatively affect the health of consumers who draw a conclusion based on its message. You will then create a public service message that would prevent the ad from having a negative impact on young adolescents. Follow these steps to work through this project:

1. Choose a type of ad and have each group member fill in the "Advertisement-Consequences Web." Choose a generic category such as jeans rather than choosing a specific brand of jeans. You may make up a name brand, but this is not necessary. You may browse through the materials at this station to think of ideas.
2. Work as a group to choose one of the effects or arguments (B or C from the Web) that you'd like to use for your public service message.
3. Decide on a format for your message from the list below. If you have other ideas, request permission to use an alternate idea.
   - Television commercial
   - Radio commercial
   - Cartoon strip
   - News report
4. Get a Storyboard Handout (one per person) and create a storyboard for your chosen format of delivery. Be sure to include the following:
   - Type of ad—Be sure your audience knows what type of ad is being targeted.
   - Possible negative outcome. Convey this through acting (commercials), discussing (news report), or drawing (cartoon strip).
   - Counter argument to extinguish the negative outcome .Convey this through acting (commercials), discussing (news report), or drawing (cartoon strip).
5. If props will improve your message, obtain or make them.
6. Prepare to present your public service message to the class. If it is a commercial or news report, practice acting it out.

Student Directions:

Advertisement-Consequences Web

1. In box A, list the type of ad your group has chosen (examples include jeans, cigarettes, fast cars, skateboarding, etc.).
2. In each box B, list a negative effect that may result if an adolescent views your selected ad. You need two different effects. For example, if you chose "jeans," one effect could be that the ad portrays the idea that the viewer must be skinny to wear these jeans, and the viewer may develop an eating disorder. The other effect may be that this particular brand of jeans is preferred above others, and they must be purchased regardless of whether or not the buyer can afford them.
3. In box C, list an argument that could be used to prevent the effect (box B) from occurring. For example, for the first example in step #2, a person could argue that models who wear the jeans in the ad are not the weight of an average person.

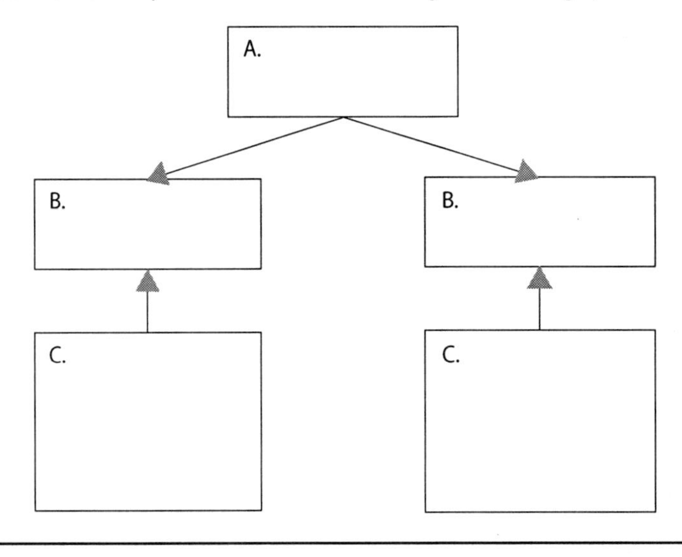

Assessment and evaluation

Use the Audience Guide and the Grading Rubric (p. 43) to assess and evaluate students' progress. The Audience Guide is for student use during skit performances. When scoring it, consider that one of its purposes is to promote active listening in order to engage students in interpreting each of the public service messages. Students who identify appropriate outcomes, arguments, and applications for all messages may qualify for the "exceptional" rating, and those who have some appropriate responses may qualify as "average."

Audience Guide for Public Service Messages

Advertisement	Possible Negative Outcome	Counter Argument	How This Applies to My Life

Public Service Messages Grading Rubric

	Needs Improvement	Average	Exceptional
Individual Assessment			
Overall contribution to group	1	2	3
Advertisement-Consequences Web	1	2	3
Audience Guide for Public Service Messages	1	2	3
Group Assessment			
Type of ad is indicated without using a real name brand	1	2	3
Possible negative outcome is presented and easily identifiable	1	2	3
Counter argument is presented and easily identifiable	1	2	3
Overall quality of public service message	1	2	3
Ability to work together	1	2	3

Teacher Comments:

Literacy station #1: Outlining with clay

Related to IRA/NCTE Standard:

6: *Students apply knowledge of language structure, language conventions (e.g., spelling and punctuation), media techniques, figurative language, and genre to create, critique, and discuss print and nonprint texts. (International Reading Association and the National Council of Teachers of English, 1996)*

The purpose of this station is to make the format of outlining (parallel construction and the use of letters or numerals and their form) explicit to students who are often quite confused by it. To place all of the emphasis on the format, no content is added to the outline; rather, the goal is to develop a framework of an outline by choosing where to place various levels of the topics, subtopics, and ideas.

Materials and preparation

1. Obtain a packet of modeling clay. (If you get the type that will not dry out, you will only need one packet, as it will be reused for each group.)
2. Decide on a work area. A long table works best. Because the clay may leave smudge marks on the table, you may choose to cover the table with old butcher paper or an inexpensive tablecloth.
3. Prepare student directions and scoring guide (see samples, p. 45). Review the guide with students before they begin work at the station.

Assessment and evaluation

As you circulate, observe students as they make decisions about the order and placements of numerals and letters. Record difficulties in your anecdotal notes, but take advantage of any teachable moments to briefly review the format of outlines. The scoring guide can be used as a graded evaluation, or it can simply be used as a basis for a contest among groups. The following guidelines may be used to determine total points:

Parallel construction: If it is perfect, the group earns the full 20 points. Deduct 5 points for each error.

Number of lines: Award one point for each line (row) in the format up to 20 points, or if the score can be greater than 100, award one point for each line.

Number of levels: Award 5 points for each level in the outline. For example, the outline on p. 45 has three levels and would earn 15 points.

Periods (one point off for each missing): Groups earn the full 20 points if they include a period after each letter and numeral.

Group's ability to work cooperatively: If the group works up to your expectations, award them with the 20 points. If not, take off 5 points for each infraction.

Student Directions:

Clay Outline Format

I. Work as a group.
  A. Create one format as a group.
  B. All group members must help.
II. Task
  A. Create an outline format.
    1. Use many levels.
    2. Use parallel construction.
    3. You are only making the frame of the outline. There will be no words in it.
  B. Use clay.
    1. Make letters and numerals.
    2. Use a mat under the clay.
    3. Don't get clay on the floor!
III. Scoring.
  A. When complete, get [teacher's name] to score it.
  B. See scoring guide below.

Scoring Guide

	Possible Score	Your Score
Parallel Construction	20	
Number of lines	20	
Number of levels	20	
Periods (one point off for each one missing)	20	
Group's ability to work cooperatively	20	

Total = __________ __________

Literacy station #2: Paper bag skits

Related to IRA/NCTE Standards:

4. *Students adjust their use of spoken, written, and visual language (e.g., conventions, style, vocabulary) to communicate effectively with a variety of audiences and for different purposes.*
5. *Students employ a wide range of strategies as they write and use different writing process elements appropriately to communicate with different audiences for a variety of purposes.*
11. *Students participate as knowledgeable, reflective, creative, and critical members of a variety of literacy communities.*
12. *Students use spoken, written, and visual language to accomplish their own purposes—for learning, enjoyment, persuasion, and the exchange of information. (International Reading Association/National Council of Teachers of English, 1996)*

This station engages students in a highly interactive activity that enhances their understanding of story structure and story elements. A paper bag containing five props stimulates their developing original skits. Using interactive tools from ReadWriteThink or a graphic organizer, students map out the story elements of their skits. As students view other groups' performances and determine the conflicts and resolutions of each, students practice listening and critical thinking skills. Groups will need at least two class periods to complete this station followed by a whole-class day of performing their skits (A whole-class expanded version of this lesson is available at http://www.readwritethink.org/lessons/lesson_view.asp?id=1024. *

Materials and preparation

1. Prepare the paper bag; only one bag is needed because all groups use the same bag, and its size will be determined by the size of the items you include in it. Inside the bag, place five seemingly random items students will use as props in the skits. Examples of objects you might include are: baseball cap, ticket stub, map, travel brochure, keys, newspaper article, sunglasses, winter scarf, and photograph.
2. Decide how your students will create their graphic organizers. If the group can have access to a computer, the ReadWriteThink's Drama Map interactive student tool is ideal (www.readwritethink.org/materials/dramamap/). This digital tool leads students through character development, setting, conflict,

* The lesson "Developing Story Structure with Paper-Bag Skits" was written by Nancy Kolodziej and published on ReadWriteThink.org, a Thinkfinity website developed by the International Reading Association, the National Council of Teachers of English, and in partnership with the Verizon Foundation.

and resolution. If a computer is not available, you can supply students with a graphic organizer on which they may develop these story elements. Scholastic (http://www2.scholastic.com/browse/article.jsp?id=2983) has many free graphic organizers that can be used for this task. Consider using the "Story Map" handout or browse through the many other free graphic organizers, which may be found online by using "free graphic organizer," "free story map," or "free story elements graphic organizer" as your search phrases. Because this station focuses on story elements and the conflict and resolution of the plot in particular, be sure to select a story map that includes these items and requires students to complete all items on the story map prior to beginning to compose their skits (see Step 5 of the Student Directions).

3. Prepare student directions (see sample, p. 48).
4. Create a Cooperative Group Roles handout (see sample, p. 48)
5. Create a Guidelines for Creating and Performing Skits (see sample, p. 49).
6. Create a Conflict-Resolution Audience Guide (see sample, p. 49). Use this to focus students' attention on the conflict and resolution of each skit during the whole-class presentations.

Assessment and evaluation

A rubric (p. 50) is provided for assessing the skit, written work, on-task behaviors, and guidelines described in the student directions. Discussing the rubric with students as you introduce the station will encourage them to stay on task and meet expectations.

The "Conflict-Resolution Audience Guide" (see sample, p. 49) is for student use during skit performances. When scoring it, consider that one of its purposes is to promote active listening. Students who independently identify the correct conflict and resolution in all of the skits may qualify for the "exceptional" rating, and those who correct their answers during the review of the conflict and resolution of each skit may qualify as "acceptable." When evaluating student responses on this guide, be sure to consider the clarity of each skit. If it is difficult to determine these elements in a particular skit, allow for flexibility in the students' responses.

Student Directions:

Paper Bag Skits

Create a skit that your group will perform for our class. You will develop your skit based on details you include on a story map. Follow these directions to complete the assignment:
—Adapted with permission from ReadWriteThink (Kolodziej, 2006)

1. Using the handout below, assign each member of your group a role.
2. Read the Guidelines for Creating and Performing Skits.
3. Remove the items from the bag.
4. These items will be the props that you will use in your skit.
5. Brainstorm possible stories that can be developed using all five props. Your skit must not contain violence or inappropriate language or actions.
6. On the computer, go to http://www.readwritethink.org/materials/dramamap/. Complete all of the items in the story map to create the framework of your skit. Each group member must have a role in the skit. (It is acceptable to include a role of Narrator.)
7. Print your maps. You will hand these in when you perform your skit.
8. Compose a skit based on your story map and rehearse it. Be sure that your conflict and resolution are able to be identified by your audience. Remember to use all of the props from the bag and easily heard, clear voices.
9. At the end of the class period, return all props to the bag.

Paper Bag Skit Cooperative Group Roles (Kolodziej, 2006)

1. Determine each group member's month of birth and list each name in order from January to December.

   a. ______________ b. ______________

   c. ______________ d. ______________

   e. ______________ f. ______________

   Note: If there are only 4 people in your group, Member C will perform both the *c* and the *d* tasks. If there are 6 members, Member F will share the Recorder role.

2. To determine each member's task, match each letter from above to its capital listed below. For example, Member A will be the Facilitator

   A. Facilitator—Coordinates the group. Helps to ensure that each group member participates in all of the activities and that the group remains on task. Prints and retains the drama maps. Brings them to class daily so they may be turned in at the appropriate time.

   B. Director—Focuses on character movement and voice during the skit and gives suggestions.

   C. Casting Director—Makes suggestions for filling roles based on group members' attributes.

   D. Screenwriter—Suggests possible character lines.

   E. Recorder—Writes brainstormed ideas and enters data into the drama map.

Guidelines for Creating and Performing Skits

Creating your skit

- Each group member must have a role in the skit. (It is acceptable to include a role of Narrator in your skit.)
- You must use all of the items in your bag as props.
- Your skit must not contain violence or inappropriate language or actions.
- While using the Internet, you may access only the ReadWriteThink.org website.

Performing and viewing skits

- Use clear voices that can be easily heard.
- Be a polite audience. Put-downs are not permitted.

Student Directions:

Conflict-Resolution Audience Guide (Kolodziej, 2006)

After each performance (except for your own group), record the conflict and resolution in the appropriate columns. Write "My Group" when your group performs. **Please do not write during performances.**

	Conflict	Resolution
Group 1		
Group 2		
Group 3		
Group 4		
Group 5		
Group 6		
Group 7		

Paper Bag Skits Grading Rubric (Kolodziej, 2006)

	Needs Improvement	Average	Exceptional
Individual Assessment			
Completion of group member role	1	2	3
Overall contribution to group	1	2	3
Adherence to guidelines	1	2	3
Conflict-Resolution Audience Guide	1	2	3
Group Assessment			
Drama Map	1	2	3
Use of props	1	2	3
Skit	1	2	3
Ability to work together	1	2	3

Teacher Comments:

Mathematics station #1: The locker problem

Related to NCTM Standards:

1. *Number and Operations*
2. *Algebra*
6. *Problem Solving*
7. *Reasoning and Proof*
8. *Communication*
10. *Representation*

(National Council of Teachers of Mathematics, 2000)

This famous problem engages students in interactive problem solving. Because this is a difficult problem, some of your groups may not solve the problem before the end of the period. You may consider having a whole-class discussion after every group has worked on the problem. I suggest that you have each group discuss the strategies and models they used and the rationales for their responses.

Materials and preparation

1. Create a Locker Problem Handout (see sample, p. 52)
2. Create locker board manipulatives. You will need one for each pair of students. Place the locker boards in a large envelope. Label the envelope "Do not open until the directions ask you to do so" (see sample, p. 53)
3. Prepare student directions (see sample, p. 53).

Assessment and evaluation

Assess students' problem-solving skills and rationales provided for answers. The solution to the problem is that the lockers that would remain open are lockers 1, 4, 9, 16, 25, 36, 49, 64, 81, and 100. These are all perfect squares. For more information about this problem and applet tools to accompany it, run an Internet search with the term "locker problem." There are many excellent resources containing explanations and applets. One of my favorite sites is the Connected Math Project's (http://connectedmath.msu.edu/CD/Grade6/Locker/#instructions), which includes an applet to demonstrate the actions of opening and closing lockers. The Math Forum also has a helpful site (http://mathforum.org/alejandre/frisbie/locker.html) and explains various approaches that students can use to solve this problem.

The Locker Problem Handout

Imagine that you are looking down a hallway that contains 100 lockers. Each locker has its door shut. A line of 100 students has formed at the beginning of that hallway.

1. The first student walks down the line of lockers and opens every locker.
2. The second student walks down the line of lockers and, beginning with the second locker, closes each second locker.
3. The third student walks down the line and, beginning with the third locker, changes the state of every third locker. (In other words, if the locker is open, he closes it; if it is closed, he opens it.)
4. The fourth person walks down the line, and beginning with the fourth locker, changes the state of every fourth locker.
5. This pattern continues until all 100 students have passed down the line of lockers.

The problem:
After the 100th student passes by the lockers, which of the lockers will be open?

1. What are you trying to solve in this problem?
2. What models (drawings, manipulatives, etc.) could you use to help you solve this problem? How will you use them?
3. (Answer this question after removing the locker boards from the envelope.) How can you use the locker boards to help you solve this problem?
4. (Once you think you have solved the problem, answer this question.) After the 100th student passes by the lockers, which lockers will be open?
5. Why does your answer to question #4 make sense?

Locker Board Manipulatives

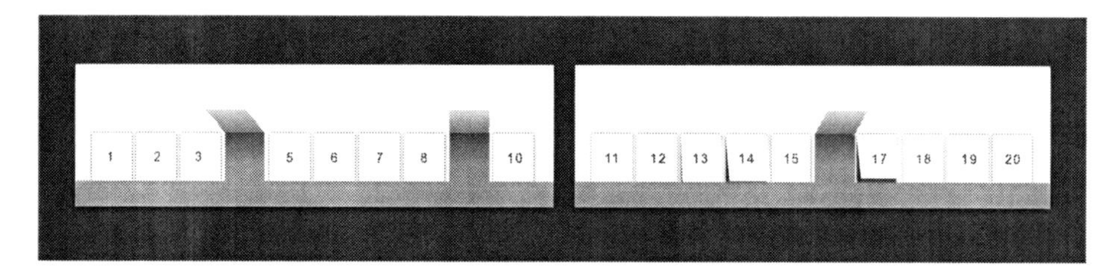

Student Directions:

Locker Board

Goal: To use logical thinking and various mathematical strategies to solve a problem.

Directions:

1. Read the Locker Problem handout.
2. Discuss and answer questions 1 and 2 on the handout.
3. Open the envelope and remove the locker boards.
4. Discuss and complete question 3.
5. Work through the locker problem using any strategies and models that will help you solve the problem.
6. Once you think you have solved the problem, or if you run out of time, discuss and complete questions 4 and 5 on the handout.
7. Place your handout in the Papers Handed In tray.
8. Please do not share your strategy or solution with other groups. Allow them the opportunity to work through this challenging problem.

Mathematics station #2: Math curse

Related to NCTM Standards:

1. *Number and Operations*
2. *Algebra*
3. *Geometry*
4. *Measurement*
5. *Data Analysis and Probability*
6. *Problem Solving*
8. *Communication*
9. *Connections*
10. *Representation*

(National Council of Teachers of Mathematics, 2000)

Math phobia is common among many students; unfortunately, it is a problem often carried over into their adult lives. One goal of this station is to eradicate that stance by showing students that math is prevalent in all aspects of our lives. Students will read the book *Math Curse* (Scieszka, 1995) and then create their own "math curses."

Materials and preparation

1. Obtain the book, *Math Curse*. Read it so that you are familiar with the structure of the story.
2. Create the student directions (see sample, p. 55).
3. Create a rubric (see sample, p. 56) and photocopy one per student. Discuss this rubric with students before they begin the station to help them meet expectations. At some point, the students will be ready to help create rubrics, a proper step in having them assume more responsibility for their own educations.

Student Directions:

Math Curse

Many people have phobias of math, and during this station you will read about one girl who overcame her phobia after encountering many "math curses" in her daily life. After reading the book, you'll create your own math curse; but the setting for your curses will be (your school's name) Middle School.

1. Give each person in your group a Math Curse handout.
2. Within your group, choose your roles for this project.

   Facilitator: Organizes the reading of the book.

   Scribe: Writes ideas generated by the group (brainstormed list, draft of curses, etc.).

   Editor: Ensures that all guidelines of the project are followed, particularly the criteria for the curses.

   Presenter: Shares your group's curses with the class
3. Read the book together. You can take turns reading pages, choose one person to read the whole book, or choose your own method to read it. You won't have time to solve the problems today, but we will work some of them out as a whole class on another day.
4. Brainstorm a list of possible places and types of "math curses" people may encounter at (your school's name) Middle School.
5. Based on your list from Step 4, write three "math curses." Each curse must:
   a. Begin with stating a location (example: *You are walking into the office when…*).
   b. Have at least two steps (example: *the principal stops you and asks you if you have time to walk a visitor to the cafeteria. You look at the clock, and see that it is now 11:35. If it takes you two minutes to walk to the cafeteria, and your appointment with the guidance counselor is at 11:40, do you have enough time to escort the visitor?*)
   c. End with a mathematical question that readers can solve. You may insert appropriate humorous curses in your presentation, but they will not count towards your three mathematical curses.
6. You will create a PowerPoint slide for each curse. Add graphics to make it visually appealing.
7. Look over the grading rubric before you begin; and when you think you are finished, confirm that you have met all criteria.
8. Be ready to present your curses in class.

Student Directions:

***Math Curse* Rubric**

Self-assessment: Rate your work on each of the criteria listed in the chart by checking the appropriate column.

Criteria	Basic: 1 point	Average: 2 points	Exceptional: 3 points
I fulfilled my group role to the best of my ability.			
I worked cooperatively with my group.			
My group's curses follow all guidelines.			

Teacher Assessment:

Criteria	Basic: 1 point	Average: 2 points	Exceptional: 3 points
Curse #1			
Curse #2			
Curse #3			
PowerPoint display			
Completed on time			

Assessment and evaluation

The teacher and the student will evaluate this assignment independently. Place a copy of the rubric above with the station materials so students may refer to it as they begin their assignment. To rate each of the products and processes on the rubric, consider that "average" would be earned for those that meet your expectations, "exceptional" would be earned for those that exceed your expectations, and "basic" would denote those that fall below your expectations.

Music station: Identify these songs

Related to MENC Music Standards:

5. *Reading and notating music.*
6. *Listening to, analyzing, and describing music.*

(Consortium of National Arts Education, 1994)

Many adolescents are all-but-addicted to popular music. However, these students are often indifferent toward music class. This center helps students connect content learned in music class to their interest in popular music as they apply their knowledge of reading sheet music to identify popular songs.

Materials and preparation

1. Choose three to five songs to be used in this center. To gain optimal student interest in the center, choose currently popular songs. Ask your students to suggest songs that you can use, making sure to screen them for inappropriate language and content.
2. Obtain sheet music for the songs. Most sheet music is available online, and it is possible to get it for free. To find possible sources, type "free sheet music" in your search engine.
3. Choose a popular segment of the song; consider using the chorus.
4. Make a copy of the segment's music and lyrics; this will be the answer key.
5. White out the lyrics on a second copy of the chosen segment, label it *Song A* (or *B, C,* etc.), and make four photocopies. (If you would like to make the pages more durable, laminate them or photocopy them on card stock.) Follow steps 3-5 for each of the chosen songs.
6. Create the student directions (see sample, p. 58). Adjust Item #3 to indicate targeted vocabulary in your curriculum.
7. Create the student handout (see sample, p. 58).
8. Type a list of the song titles in random order and put this list in an envelope labeled "Hints."

Assessment and evaluation

Use students' responses on the handout to assess and evaluate progress towards understanding. In particular, look for proper use of key vocabulary (as indicated in #3 of the Student Directions).

Student Directions:

Identify These Songs

The sheet music at this station contains the chorus of popular songs that you might hear on (list a local radio station that plays the type of music you selected). Your challenge is to read the music notation to try to determine the title of each song. Don't look in the "Hint" envelope until Step 5 below.

1. Write your name on a Student Handout (one per person).
2. Choose one of the pages of sheet music and give each person a copy of it.
3. Discuss and complete Student Handout items 1-3 for Song A. Be sure to include terms such as *pitch, timbre, beats, meter,* etc.
4. Repeat the steps for songs B and C.
5. Check the "Hint" envelope to see whether the song titles you chose are on the list.
6. Write your final guess of each song title.
7. Put your paper in the Papers Handed In slot.

Identify These Songs: Student Handout

Song A

1. What is the tempo of this song? What specific evidence supports this conclusion?
2. Describe the melody of the song.
3. What song do you think this is?
4. After looking at the "Hints," we think this song is:

Song B

1. What is the tempo of this song? What specific evidence supports this conclusion?
2. Describe the melody of the song.
3. What song do you think this is?
4. After looking at the "Hints," we think this song is:

Song C

1. What is the tempo of this song? What specific evidence supports this conclusion?
2. Describe the melody of the song.
3. What song do you think this is?
4. After looking at the "Hints," we think this song is:

Science station #1: Magic square vocabulary

Related to NRC Science Standards:

1. *Unifying concepts and processes in science*
2. *Science as Inquiry*
3. *Physical Science*
4. *Life Science*
5. *Earth and Space Science*

(National Research Council, 1996)

The magic square activity can be used with nearly any subject area and for varied purposes. It can serve as an introductory activity when beginning a new unit or topic and also works well as a review strategy. When using a magic square, give your students a few minutes to work independently. Then, have them work in small groups to compare thoughts and complete the square. This group interaction generates much discussion about the terms and how they compare and contrast with one another. This station can be used to review critical academic vocabulary in preparation for a state science assessment. The terms and some of their definitions were retrieved from the "Tennessee Academic Vocabulary for Sixth Grade: Science" page of the *State Improvement Grant: Tennessee Academic Vocabulary* website (http://sig.cls.utk.edu/TAV/default.htm).

Materials and preparation

1. Choose vocabulary terms.
2. Create a Magic Squares Puzzle handout (see sample, p. 60). Photocopy one per student.
3. Create student directions (see sample, p. 61).
4. Create word cards for charades. Write each term from the Magic Square handout on small pieces of paper. Fold these up and place them in a bucket or basket. Students will draw words for charades from this bucket.

Student Directions:

Magic Squares Puzzle

Match the terms in Part A with their definitions in Part B by placing the number in its corresponding letter box in Part C. If the totals of the numbers are the same both across the rows and down the columns in each possible direction, you have found the magic number. If your totals do not add up to the same number in each column and row, find your errors and correct your work.

Part A

A. COMMENSALISM

B. MUTUALISM

C. PARASITISM

D. PRODUCER

E. CONSUMER

F. DECOMPOSER

G. WAVE LENGTH

H. AMPLITUDE

I. FREQUENCY

Part B

1. The number of cycles in a wave during a period of time.
2. A photosynthetic plant would be classified as one of these.
3. A relationship between two organisms; both benefit and neither is harmed.
4. An animal that feeds on other plants or animals.
5. A relationship between two organisms; one feeds off of the other and causes it harm.
6. The distance between two successive points in a wave.
7. Describes a relationship between two organisms; one feeds off the other, and the other one is not harmed.
8. The difference between a zero value and the maximum value in a wavelength.
9. An organism that causes dead plants or animals to decay.

Part C

A	B	C
D	E	F
G	H	I

Indicate the magic number ___________

Student Directions:

Magic Squares

The purpose of this station is to review key science terms in preparation for our state assessment. During this station, you will complete a "Magic Squares" puzzle and then create charades to illustrate each of the terms on the puzzle.

1. Each person must independently complete a Magic Squares puzzle.
2. After everyone has finished, compare answers. Discuss and fix inconsistencies.
3. For each term, compose a charade to demonstrate its meaning.
4. Quietly, so that other groups don't see or hear your ideas, practice the charades.
5. Charades will later be used to play a game with the class. Place your Magic Squares Puzzle in your science notebook. You will need to refer to this when we play charades.

Assessment and evaluation

Informally assess students during the charades game. To play the game, arrange students so they are sitting near their station group members. Groups should choose team leaders. Take turns calling on groups to come to the front of the room and randomly take a paper from the bucket or basket of word cards. Give each group one minute to organize its charade. As groups perform their charades, the rest of the class watches. Groups meet and quietly decide on their answers. A group member writes it on a dry erase board or blank piece of paper. Each group with the correct answer earns a point, and the performing group wins a point if at least one group guesses its charade.

Science station #2: Closed circuits

Related to NRC Science Standards

1. *Unifying concepts and processes in science*
2. *Science as inquiry*
3. *Physical Science*
6. *Science and Technology*

(National Research Council, 1996)

Materials and preparation

This inquiry-based lesson prompts students to self-discover the theory of closed circuits. Students make conjectures and test them in an interactive hands-on approach. Writing in science learning logs is also incorporated. This station was adapted from the "How Can You Construct a Circuit in Which a Bulb Lights?" activity in Carin, Bass, and Contant's *Teaching Science as Inquiry* (2005, pp. A124–A127). Another excellent resource, "Experiment 6—Electric Light Bulb Experiment" (Bakersfield College) is available online (http://www2.bc.cc.ca.us/dkimball/Physical%20Science/New%20Labs/Exp%206%20Light%20Bulbs%20and%20Circuits.pdf). This website includes a helpful student handout with diagrams of various configurations of a light bulb, batteries, and wires (p. 39). Be sure to note, however, that the some of the diagrams on the handout include two wires and/or two light bulbs. Consequently, it may be considered as a follow-up station to the one described here.

1. Obtain supplies. Each student will need two 12" pieces of 12-gauge wire (strip ¼" of insulation from each end), one D battery, and one flashlight bulb.
2. Create student directions (see sample, p. 63).

Assessment and evaluation

Take anecdotal notes of students' problem-solving strategies as they work through this project. Assess student logs and prediction sheets for level of understanding of closed circuits.

Student Directions:

Closed Circuit: Student Directions

The Scenario: Because a major hurricane is headed to our area, the [your school district's name] School District has decided to retain all students at school until the storm passes. It is now dark outside, when suddenly, the power goes out. No flashlights are available, but you remember that Mr. [insert teacher name here] has batteries, light bulbs, and wire in his classroom and said they could be useful during a power failure. Unfortunately, he is absent today, so you are on your own to try to produce some light.

1. Open up your science log and label the next blank page with the date and title of this station.
2. Write your materials list: 2 wires, 1 light bulb, and 1 D battery.
3. Write this problem statement in your log: *How can I light a bulb with just one wire and one battery?*
4. Write your hypothesis by completing this statement: *I think that I can light the bulb by* ______________________. (How do you think you will light the bulb?)
5. Label the next section of your log *Process*. Draw and write about each of your attempts as you work through the rest of this project.
6. Get your materials. You need two wires and ONLY one light bulb and D battery.
7. Try to light the bulb. Draw each new strategy in your log, showing the placement of your bulb, battery, and wire.
8. Once you get the bulb to light, label the next section of your log *Solution*. Draw a picture of your method for lighting the bulb, showing the placement of your bulb, battery, and wire. Describe this method below your drawing.
9. Get another wire.
10. Write this problem statement in your log: *How can I light a bulb with TWO wires and one battery, WITHOUT the bulb touching the battery?*
11. Work through steps 4 through 8.
12. Place your log in the Papers Handed In slot.

Social studies station #1: *Esperanza Rising*

Related to NCSS Standards:

1. *Culture*
2. *Time, Continuity, and Change*
3. *People, Places, and Environment*
4. *Individuals, Groups, and Institutions*
8. *Global Connections*

(National Council for the Social Studies, 1994)

This station develops background knowledge as students explore Aguascalientes, Mexico, and Salinas Valley, California, using Google Earth. Students will also learn about migrant camp culture by visiting a website. An anticipation guide will assess prior knowledge and focus students' attention on key ideas. This station was developed to help students comprehend the novel *Esperanza Rising* (Munoz Ryan, 2001) while learning social studies content (see p. 23 for more information about using this novel to integrate instruction). Because of the nature of some of the open-ended items on the anticipation guide, a whole-class discussion should ensue after all students have completed this station.

Materials and preparation

1. Coordinate implementation of this station with the language arts teacher so that when students read this novel in language arts class, you focus on social studies standards through the use of its content. Start the station after students have started reading *Esperanza Rising*.
2. Bookmark websites on student computers. You will need a computer for each pair of students at the station.
   a. Encyclopedia Britannica (http://www.britannica.com/eb/article-9004095/Aguascalientes)
   b. Salinas Chamber of Commerce (http://www.salinaschamber.com/living_here.asp)
   c. Weedpatch Camp (http://www.weedpatchcamp.com/index.htm)

3. If Google Earth is not on the computers, download and install it. A free download is available at Google Earth (http://earth.google.com/). Place a shortcut to this program on the desktop of each computer. Open Google Earth and enter Aguascalientes, Mexico, in the "fly to" window. A blue link to Aguascalientes will appear in the window below the "fly to" window. Click and drag this link to the "Places" window just below its current location. Students will be able to simply click on this link to get to the location on the map. You can also change the speed that it "flies" from one place to another. To do so, choose the "Tools" menu, then the "Options" link, click on "Touring," and move the slide button close to "Slow." If you place it all the way on "Slow," it moves much too slowly.
4. Create the Anticipation Guide (see sample p. 66) and photocopy one per student.
5. Create the Student Directions (see sample, p. 67).

Assessment and evaluation

Review student responses in the "After Viewing and Reading" and "Evidence and Thoughts" columns of the Anticipation Guides to check for accuracy. Note that those items requiring a personal response may not result in uniform responses. These items provide the basis for a good class discussion.

Student Directions:

Anticipation Guide for *Esperanza Rising*

	Before Viewing and Reading		After Viewing and Reading		Evidence and Thoughts
	Agree	Disagree	Agree	Disagree	
1. Aguascalientes remains a rural ranch community today.					
2. Literally, Aguascalientes translates "hot water." It got this name because of hot springs located there.					
3. Today, Aguascalientes is difficult to reach because it does not have an airport or train station.					
4. Salinas remains a rural farming community today.					
5. I would like to live in the Salinas Valley area.					
6. Migrant farmer camps no longer exist.					
7. Life in the federal migrant camps was better than life in most of the farmers' migrant camps.					
8. In the past, migrant camp children were treated unfairly in school.					
9. A pair of shoes was a luxury for migrant camp children.					

Student Directions:

Esperanza Rising Station

You've been reading *Esperanza Rising* in your language arts class. This station will link what you have been learning to social studies content. You'll focus on geographical, cultural, and economical factors in Aguascalientes, the Salinas Valley, and a migrant camp. The camp, Weedpatch Camp, is very close in distance to the camp in which Pam Muñoz Ryan's grandmother lived, but it is not the same one.

1. Give each person an Anticipation Guide. Work independently to fill in the Before Viewing and Reading column by placing a checkmark to indicate whether you agree or disagree with each statement. Your responses do not have to be correct. You'll have a chance later on to change your mind.
2. After everyone's Anticipation Guide is completed, move to the computers. You will work in groups of two for this segment. Depending on your class size, you may have a group of three at one computer.
3. On the desktop, click on Google Earth to open this tool.
4. In the Google Earth window, double click on Aguascalientes. The map will display this area. Zoom in and out to view the area as it looks in current times.
5. In the "Fly To" window, enter "Salinas, CA," and you will "fly" to this location. Again, zoom in and out to view the area as it looks in current times.
6. Open the web browser and choose Encyclopedia Britannica (http://www.britannica.com/eb/article-9004095/Aguascalientes) from the bookmarks.
7. Read the brief entry about Aguascalientes. Complete the "After Viewing and Reading" and "Evidence and Thoughts" columns for items #1-3 on your Anticipation Guide. Be sure to include proof of your response in the Evidence and Thoughts column.
8. Choose the Salinas Chamber of Commerce bookmark (http://www.salinaschamber.com/living_here.asp), and read this brief overview of the Salinas Valley area. Complete the "After Viewing and Reading" and "Evidence and Thoughts" columns for items #4 and 5 on your Anticipation Guide.
9. Choose the Weedpatch Camp bookmark (http://www.weedpatchcamp.com/index.htm).
   a. Click on and read these pages: "Opening Page," "Weedpatch Camp History," "Life in the Camp," "The Federal Role," "Weedpatch School," and "Personal Reminiscences: Shelton Family."
   b. Complete the rest of your Anticipation Guide.
10. Meet with the rest of your group and compare responses. Adjust any that you think should be changed.
11. Place your paper in the Papers Handed In bin.

Social studies station #2: Vocabulary word sort

Related to NCSS Standards

1. *Culture*
2. *Time, Continuity, and Change*
7. *Science, Technology, and Society*

(National Council for the Social Studies, 1994)

Word sorts are excellent vocabulary development and review activities. They are more effective than written worksheets because the word cards allow students to easily manipulate the words, and they can test ideas and change their minds without having to erase and rewrite words. In a closed word sort, the teacher provides the categories that will be used. In an open word sort, however, the teacher does not supply the categories; they are generated by the students. Afterwards, groups discuss the categories they chose and their rationale for these choices. Word sorts can be used to introduce a new topic or to review vocabulary words and concepts. This station's closed word sort is meant to be an introduction to the topic of the castle life in the Middle Ages. You can easily adapt this station for any subject and topic by simply changing the words on the word cards.

Materials and preparation

1. Determine the vocabulary words for the sort.
2. Create word cards (see the *Assessment and evaluation* section for words). Either write them on 3 x 5 index cards or print them onto more durable card stock. You will need two or three sets of cards for the station. Place each set of cards in a large envelope or plastic zipper bag and label it "Middle Ages Vocabulary Word Sort."
3. Create category headings. It is helpful to use a different color card stock or index card for these. Another option is to use larger cards for these headings.
4. Create the student directions (see sample, p. 69). It may be helpful to print extra copies of this and place them with each set of word cards.

Student Directions:

Middle Ages Vocabulary Word Sort

1. You will work in groups of two for this activity. If your group has an odd number of people, you will need to make one group of three.
2. Each group should take a Middle Ages Vocabulary Word Sort envelope.
3. You will need room to spread out all of the cards. Find a space at a table or on the floor, or create a place.
4. Remove the words from the envelope and spread them out.
5. Read the words (don't worry about pronunciation right now), and try to guess what some of their meanings may be. You will be unfamiliar with many of the words. Don't worry. This will not be graded. I will use your work to determine how much knowledge you already possess about castle life in the Middle Ages.
6. You will find three cards that look different from the others and are labeled "Entertainment," "People," and "Castle Parts." These are the headings of the categories of your cards. Place them at the top of your workspace.
7. Sort your cards under each of the headings. When you are unsure of where to place a word, discuss it and make a good guess.
8. When you have all of your words categorized, get a piece of notebook paper (one per person) and a pencil. Write your name on your paper.
9. Fold your paper into thirds. It doesn't matter which way you hold your paper.
10. Copy your headings and your cards onto your paper.
11. Place your paper in the "Papers Handed In" bin.

Assessment and evaluation

The purpose of this station is to activate and assess students' prior knowledge of castle life in the Middle Ages. Use the papers handed in to informally assess this knowledge. Return the papers to students so they may keep them in their notebooks and take notes on them throughout the unit. Following is a list of the sorted terms:

People	**Entertainment**	**Castle Parts**
knight	bowling	portcullis
serf	chess	bailey
apprentice	jousting	bastion
peasant	storytelling	turret
squire	knucklebones	battlement
crusader	feasts	keep
page	acrobatics	gatehouse
master	music	drawbridge

Interdisciplinary example: Controversial issue

Related to Standards

IRA/NCTE:

1. *Students read a wide range of print and nonprint texts to build an understanding of texts, of themselves, and of the cultures of the United States and the world; to acquire new information; to respond to the needs and demands of society and the workplace; and for personal fulfillment. Among these texts are fiction and nonfiction, classic and contemporary works.*
4. *Students adjust their use of spoken, written, and visual language (e.g., conventions, style, vocabulary) to communicate effectively with a variety of audiences and for different purposes.*
5. *Students employ a wide range of strategies as they write and use different writing process elements appropriately to communicate with different audiences for a variety of purposes.*
7. *Students conduct research on issues and interests by generating ideas and questions, and by posing problems. They gather, evaluate, and synthesize data from a variety of sources (e.g., print and nonprint texts, artifacts, people) to communicate their discoveries in ways that suit their purpose and audience.*
8. *Students use a variety of technological and information resources (e.g., libraries, databases, computer networks, video) to gather and synthesize information and to create and communicate knowledge.*

(International Reading Association/National Council of Teachers of English, 1996)

NCTM:

1. *Number and Operations*
5. *Data Analysis and Probability*
8. *Communication*
9. *Connections*
10. *Representation*

(National Council of Teachers of Mathematics, 2000)

NRC Science:

2. *Science as Inquiry*

(National Research Council, 1996)

NCSS:

1. *Culture*
4. *Individuals, Groups, and Institutions*
9. *Civic Ideals and Practices*

(National Council for the Social Studies, 1994)

This example is a set of interdisciplinary stations during which students investigate a controversial issue. By focusing on particular geographical or topical issues, it can easily be adapted to suit any middle school grade and subject area. Before beginning activities at the stations, the class would need at least two whole-class sessions. The first session would involve describing the project, brainstorming possible issues or ideas, and organizing the student groups. Once students were in groups, a discussion web (p. 72) assists students in brainstorming the two sides of their chosen issues. The next whole-class session would need to be held in the computer lab so students could seek news stories and data to support both sides of the controversial issues. Students would then need several days of station work to complete the project, with some flexibility of movement from station to station. At the conclusion of the project, students would present their "news talk shows" to the class; students in the audience would actively participate in the discussions.

Materials and preparation

1. Create Discussion Web (see sample, p. 72). Photocopy one per student.
2. Create student directions (see samples, pp. 73, 74). Note that the directions have students determine their *team*'s stance on issues. If your school is not using a team approach, change the wording so that it fits your needs. For example, your students may survey all students of their own grade level that share the same lunch period.
3. Create grading rubric (see sample, p. 75).
4. Create a talk show "set" for the presentations (chairs for the panel speakers and a microphone for a prop for the audience mediator).

Student Directions:

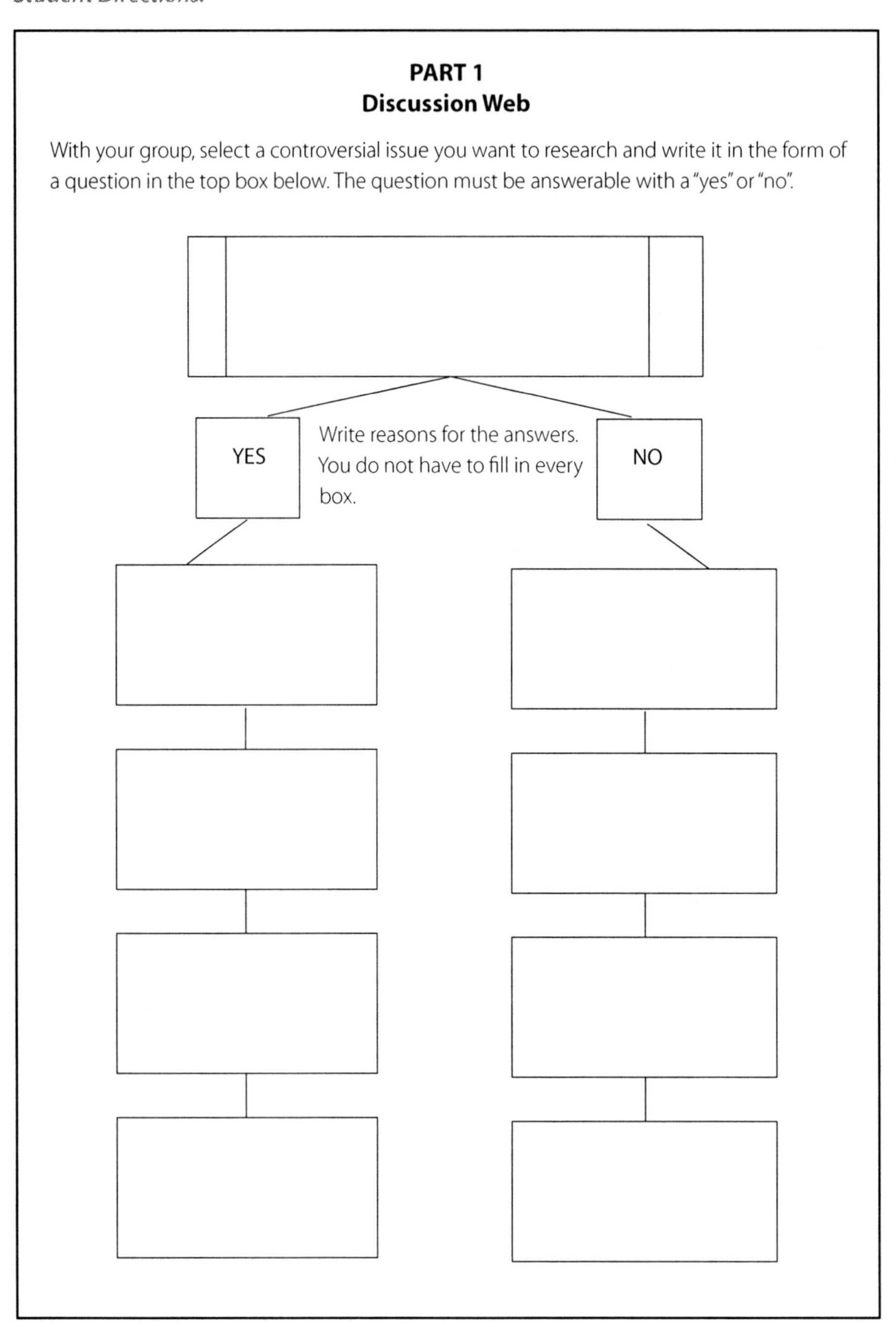

Student Directions:

PART 2

Create a Survey

Your task is to create a survey that you will administer to all the students on our team. The goal is to determine their stance on the controversial issue your group has chosen. Once you have determined your questions, create your survey on the computer, print it, and place it in the Papers Handed In slot. I'll photocopy it and return the copies to you. You must distribute them to team teachers and ask them to pass them out in homeroom the next morning. Your survey must

- Begin with an overview. Explain the purpose of your survey.
- State that the surveys are anonymous. Responders should not put names on the surveys.
- Ask at least one demographic question that pertains to your issue (Example: *Do you play sports? Do you own a cell phone? Have you always lived in this school district?*)
- Ask your controversial issue question in an impartial manner. In other words, do not indicate any bias towards one side of the issue. Include three choices: an option for each side of the issue and a neutral opinion.
- Include a brief thank you statement and your names.

Student Directions:

PART 3

Analyze Survey Data

Use your completed surveys to determine your team members' stances on the issue. Read all of the directions before you begin working.

1. Tally the number of people who chose each answer.
2. Create tables to display these data.
3. Determine percentages for each cell in the data table.
4. Include these percentages in the data table.
5. Discuss your findings. What does this mean in relation to your controversial issue?
6. Create bar graphs or pie graphs to display your data using PowerPoint.
7. Print your graphs and also save them on your flash drive.
8. The Audience Mediator will display these graphs during the introduction to your talk show.

Student Directions:

PART 4
Newspaper Article

You will work as a group to create a newspaper article in two days at this center. Please follow these guidelines:

- The first paragraph should contain the five W's (What is the issue? Who does it concern? Where is it of concern? When will it occur? Why is this an issue?).
- Paragraph 2 (or more if needed) will present one side of the argument.
- Paragraph 3 (or more if needed) will present the other side of the argument.
- The last paragraph will sum up the issue.
- Revise and edit the piece.
- Check the grading rubric to make sure your article meets the criteria.
- Type it into your word processing program.
- Proofread it.
- Place it in the Papers Handed In slot.

Student Directions:

PART 5
Talk Show Preparation and Practice

You will prepare for a "News Talk Show," which you will present in class. Although you may have decided which side of the issue you agree with, you may need to argue for the other side of the issue or appear neutral, depending on your role in this activity. You will visit this station twice.

1. Determine roles:
   a. *News Show Host:* Introduces the panel members and asks questions throughout the interview to keep the discussion going.
   b. *Audience Mediator:* Introduces the issue with brief background information and displays and explains the graph (created at the Analyze Survey Data station). During the talk show, chooses audience members who want to ask questions and state an opinion.
   c. *Panel Member A:* Sides strongly with one side of the issue and states reasons that this is the best choice.
   d. *Panel Member B:* Sides strongly with the other side of the issue.
2. Create names for your characters.
3. Prepare note cards. Create bulleted lists on index cards. Create these questions as a collaborative group. Everyone should contribute to every card.
   a. The host's card should include the panel members' names and questions to keep the discussion active.
   b. Panel members' cards should include information to support their side of the issue.
   c. Audience mediator's card will contain the introduction to the issue and graph and questions for audience members.
4. Practice your news talk show. Be ready to present it to the class.

Assessment and evaluation

Record anecdotal notes throughout this project. Use the grading rubric below, or one you create, to evaluate final work. To rate each of the products and processes on the rubric, consider that "average" would be earned for those that meet your expectations, "exceptional" would be earned for those that exceed your expectations, and "basic" would denote those that fall below your expectations.

Controversial Issue Project: Rubric

	Basic: 1	Average: 2	Exceptional: 3
Survey & Data Analysis			
Quality of survey	1	2	3
Demographic and issue question included	1	2	3
Table of data			
Percentages accurately determined	1	2	3
Fractions accurately determined	1	2	3
Bar or circle graph of data	1	2	3
Newspaper Article			
Five W's included	1	2	3
Presents both sides of issue	1	2	3
Format followed	1	2	3
Mechanics (spelling and grammar)	1	2	3
Talk Show			
Cue cards	1	2	3
Presents both sides of issue	1	2	3
Your role (individual grade)	1	2	3
Organization and preparation	1	2	3
Group's cooperative work	1	2	3

Closing Thoughts

In my 12 years of public school teaching, I taught grades K, 1, 2, 3, 7, and 8. Whenever I am asked to declare my favorite grade, I consistently reply "seventh." However, if I had been asked that question after my first year of middle school teaching, my answer would have been "first." And had I not drastically altered my style of teaching by including learning stations in the years that followed that initial year, I would continue to claim first grade as my favorite. Learning stations made all the difference for me—and my students—by providing me with the opportunity to truly get to know my students as I worked with them in small groups and in one-on-one settings. And more importantly, through learning stations I was able to meet students' physical, social, and intellectual needs. I provided learning experiences that offered opportunities for physical movement, interaction with peers, and instruction that matched each student's individual interests, learning style, and readiness level. My students became engaged and motivated learners who enjoyed my classes, and any former struggles with behavior management quickly dissipated!

Because of my tremendous success with learning stations, I was inspired to prepare this book. I hope that it will provide you with the incentive and know-how to implement learning stations in your classroom. Young adolescents deserve engaging instruction that accommodates their unique needs, makes learning enjoyable, and results in high levels of achievement. As teachers, it is our responsibility to guide our students' learning and growing as best we can—and learning stations are, at once both academically effective and developmentally responsive!

References

American Association for Health Education. (2007). *National health education standards: Achieving excellence.* Reston, VA: Author. Retrieved November 19, 2009, from http://www.aahperd.org/aahe/publications/HE-Standtard.cfm

American Council on the Teaching of Foreign Languages. (n.d.) *Standards for foreign language learning: Preparing for the 21st century, 3rd ed., Executive summary.* Alexandria, VA: Author. Retrieved August 3, 2007, from http://www.actfl.org/files/public/execsumm.pdf

Atwell, N. (1998). *In the middle: New understandings about writing, reading, and learning* (2nd ed.). Portsmouth, NH: Heinemann.

Beane, J. (2002). Beyond self-interest: A democratic core curriculum. *Educational Leadership, 59*(7), 25–28.

Beane, J. (1997). *Curriculum integration: Designing the core of democratic education.* New York: Teachers College Press.

Beane, J. (1991). The middle school: the natural home of integrated curriculum. *Educational Leadership, 49*(2), 9–13.

Ben-Ari, R., & Kedem-Friedrich, P. (2000). Restructuring heterogeneous classes for cognitive development: Social interactive perspective. *Instructional Science, 28,* 153–167.

Carin, A. A., Bass, J. E., & Contant, T. L. (2005). *Teaching science as inquiry.* Upper Saddle River, NJ: Pearson.

Committee on Nutrition. (1999). Calcium requirements of infants, children, and adolescents. *Pediatrics, 104,* 1152–1157.

Consortium of National Arts Education. (1994). *National standards for arts education: What every young American should know and be able to do in the arts.* Washington, DC: Author. Retrieved February 19, 2009, from http://artsedge.kennedy-center.org/teach/standards/

Consortium of National Arts Education. (1994). *National standards for music education.* Washington, DC: Author. Retrieved February 15, 2009, from http://artsedge.kennedy-center.org/teach/standards/standards_58.cfm#04

Erb, T. O. (Ed.) (2005). *This we believe in action.* Westerville, OH: National Middle School Association.

Erickson, H. L. (2004). Foreword. In H. H. Jacobs (Ed.), *Getting results with curriculum mapping* (pp. 1–9). Alexandria, VA: Association for Supervision and Curriculum Development.

Huebner, A. (2000). *Adolescent growth and development.* Retrieved September 9, 2009, from http://pubs.ext.vt.edu/350/350-850/350-850/

International Reading Association and the National Council of Teachers of English. (1996). *Standards for the English language arts*. Newark, DE: International Reading Association. Retrieved on August 19, 2007, from http://www.reading.org/downloads/publications/books/bk889.pdf

International Reading Association & National Middle School Association. (2001). Supporting *young adolescents' literacy learning: A joint position statement of the International Reading Association and the National Middle School Association* [Brochure]. Newark, DE: International Reading Association.

Jackson, A.W., & Davis, G.A. (2000). *Turning points 2000: Educating adolescents in the 21st century*. New York: Teachers College Press.

Jacobs, H. H. (1997). *Mapping the big picture: Integrating curriculum and assessment K–12*. Alexandria, VA: Association for Supervision and Curriculum Development.

Jacobs, H. H. (2000). Upgrading the K–12 journey through curriculum mapping. *Knowledge Quest, 29*(2), 25.

Kolodziej, N. J. (2006). Developing story structure with paper bag skits. Newark, DE: ReadWriteThink. Retrieved June 20, 2007, from http://www.readwritethink.org/lessons/lesson_view.asp?id=1024

Muñoz Ryan, P. (2001). *Esperanza rising*. Austin, TX: Holt, Rhinehart, & Winston.

National Council for the Social Studies. (1991). *Social studies in the middle school: A report of the task force on social studies in the middle school*. Silver Spring, MD: Author. Retrieved June 20, 2007, from http://www.socialstudies.org/positions/middleschool/

National Council for the Social Studies. (1994). *The curriculum standards for social studies*. Silver Spring, MD: Author. Retrieved January 24, 2007, from http://www.socialstudies.org/standards/

National Council of Teachers of English. (2006). *NCTE principles of adolescent literacy reform: A policy research brief*. Urbana, IL: Author. Retrieved November 17, 2009, from http://www.ncte.org/library/NCTEFiles/Resources/Positions/Adol-Lit-Brief.pdf

National Council of Teachers of Mathematics. (2000). *Principles & standards for school mathematics: Frequently asked questions*. Urbana, IL: Author. Retrieved June 20, 2007, from http://www.nctm.org/standards/faq.aspx

National Middle School Association. (2010). *This we believe: Keys to educating young adolescents*. Westerville, OH: Author.

National Middle School Association. (2005). *National Middle School Association's position statement on curriculum, instruction, and assessment*. Westerville, OH: Author. Retrieved October 17, 2006, from http://www.nmsa.org/AboutNMSA/PositionStatements/Curriculum/tabid/767/Default.aspx

National Middle School Association. (2003). *This we believe: Developmentally responsive middle level schools.* Westerville, OH: Author.

National Middle School Association. (2002). *NMSA position statement on curriculum integration.* Westerville, OH: Author. Retrieved November 3, 2009, from http://www.nmsa.org/AboutNMSA/PositionStatements/Curriculum Integration/tabid/282/Default.aspx

National Middle School Association. (1996). *Research summary: Young adolescents' developmental needs.* Westerville, OH: Author. Retrieved December 28, 2006, from http://www.nmsa.org/Research/ResearchSummaries/Summary5tabid/257/Default.aspx

National Research Council. (1996). *National science education standards.* Washington, DC: National Academy Press.

National Science Teachers Association. (2003). *NSTA position statement: Science education for middle level students.* Arlington, VA: Author. Retrieved June 20, 2007, from http://www.nsta.org/about/positions/middlelevel.aspx

Pipher, M. (1994). *Reviving Ophelia: Saving the selves of adolescent girls.* New York: Ballantine Books.

Powell, S. D. (2005). *Introduction to middle school.* Pearson: Upper Saddle River, NJ.

Scieszka, J. (1995). *Math curse.* New York: Viking Juvenile.

Springer, M. (2006). *Soundings: A democratic student-centered education.* Westerville, OH: National Middle School Association.

Tennessee Department of Education. (2001). *Social studies curriculum standards: Grade 6.* Nashville, TN: Author. Retrieved November 18, 2009, from http://tennessee.gov/education/curriculum.shtml

Teachers of English to Speakers of Other Languages. (n.d.). *The ESL standards for pre-k–12 students. Introduction: Promising futures.* Alexandria, VA: Author. Retrieved October 17, 2006, from http://www.tesol.org/s_tesol/sec_document.asp?CID=113&DID=310

Tomlinson, C.A. (1999). *The differentiated classroom: Responding to the needs of all learners.* Alexandria, VA: Association for Supervision and Curriculum Development.

Van Hoose, J., Strahan, D., & L'Esperance, M. (2009). *Promoting harmony: Young adolescent development & classroom practices* (3rd ed.) Westerville, OH: National Middle School Association.

Vigotsky, L. (1962). *Thought and language.* Cambridge, MA: MIT Press.

Vigotsky, L. (1978). *Mind in society.* Cambridge, MA: Harvard University Press.

Teacher Resources

Muñoz Ryan, P. (2000). *Esperanza rising*. New York: Scholastic.

Joel, B. (1998). We didn't start the fire. On *Storm Front* [CD]. New York: Sony Music.

McDill, B. (1988). Song of the South [Recorded by Alabama]. On *Southern Star* [CD]. New York: RCA Records. (1989)

Scieszka, J. (1995). *Math Curse*. New York: Viking Juvenile.

Websites Cited

Bakersfield College, Dan Kimball's Homepage, "Experiment 6 – Electric Light Bulb Experiment (http://www2.bc.cc.ca.us/dkimball/Physical%20Science/New%20Labs/Exp%206%20Light%20Bulbs%20and%20Circuits.pdf)

Connected Math Project (http://connectedmath.msu.edu/CD/Grade6/Locker/#instructions)

Discovery Education (http://school.discoveryeducation.com/lessonplans/)

Edinformatics' The Interactive Library (http://www.edinformatics.com/il/il.htm)

Encyclopedia Britannica (http://www.britannica.com/eb/article-9004095/Aguascalientes)

Google Earth (http://earth.google.com/)

iTunes (http://www.apple.com/itunes/)

Karen J. Lloyd's Storyboard Blog (http://karenjlloyd.com/blog/free-storyboard-template-downloads/)

Math Forum (http://mathforum.org/alejandre/frisbie/locker.html)

Metropolitan Museum of Art, How Van Gogh Made His Mark (http://www.metmuseum.org/explore/van_gogh/menu.html)

MusicUnited (http://www.musicunited.org/6_legalsites.html)

ReadWriteThink (http://www.readwritethink.org)

Salinas Chamber of Commerce (http://www.salinaschamber.com/living_here.asp)

Schoolhouse Video (http://www.schoolhousevideo.org/Pages/Storyboard.pdf)

Stanford University (http://fairuse.stanford.edu/Copyright_and_Fair_Use_Overview/chapter7/index.html)

State Improvement Grant: Tennessee Academic Vocabulary (http://sig.cls.utk.edu/TAV/vocab_6th_grade.html)

Utah State University's National Library of Virtual Manipulatives (http://nlvm.usu.edu/en/nav/vlibrary.html)

Verizon's Thinkfinity (http://www.thinkfinity.org/home.aspx)

Weedpatch Camp (http://www.weedpatchcamp.com/index.htm)

National Middle School Association

Since 1973, National Middle School Association (NMSA) has been the voice for those committed to the education and well-being of young adolescents and is the only national association dedicated exclusively to middle level youth.

NMSA's members are principals, teachers, central office personnel, professors, college students, parents, community leaders, and educational consultants in the United States, Canada, and 46 other countries. A major advocacy effort is Month of the Young Adolescent. This October celebration engages a wide range of organizations to help schools, families, and communities celebrate and honor young adolescents for their contributions to society.

NMSA offers publications, professional development services, and events for middle level educators seeking to improve the education and overall development of 10- to 15-year-olds. In addition to the highly acclaimed Middle School Journal, Middle Ground magazine, and Research in Middle Level Education Online, we publish more than 100 books on every facet of middle level education. Our landmark position paper, *This We Believe*, is recognized as the premier statement outlining the vision of middle level education.

Membership is open to anyone committed to the education of young adolescents. Visit **www.nmsa.org** or call **1-800-528-NMSA** for more information.

LaVergne, TN USA
15 March 2010
175939LV00003B/2/P

9 781560 902362